Bridge
Saga

Bridge Saga

The Story of the World's Greatest Players with the Hands that Made Them Immortals

Victor Mollo

HART PUBLISHING COMPANY, INC.
NEW YORK CITY

CONTENTS

CURTAIN RAISER
A preview of the past

The sun never sets on the Bridge Empire. Somewhere, every minute of every day an enthralling hand is being played. Some hands are more, much more fascinating than others, some settings are more colourful, some situations more dramatic, some players more subtle, more sophisticated, more vibrant than others, but *embarras de richesse* is the writer's only problem.

With the world as my stage and a thousand stars at my command, I can pick and choose my plays and be as fickle as I like.

To bring my theme to life, to tell the bridge story as it unfolded, day by day, during the most fateful period in the annals of the game, I have drawn on my column in London's *Evening Standard* for some two hundred illustrative hands.

History is made up of *petites histoires*, no less than of great events, the anecdotes, the intimate touches helping to bring into relief the drama and suspense. Like virtuosi, clowns and jesters and prima donnas, too, have a part to play in the broad design.

The diarist's horizons are low, but he has one advantage over the historian. Recording events as they happen, he can capture the colours before they fade, and sensing the atmosphere and the vibrations, he can convey them to the reader before the present slips into the past.

As a bridge columnist, I can make the best of both worlds—draw on the historian's wealth of material, yet record, like the diarist, every tense, dramatic moment as it occurs.

If I fail, I have no excuse, for I have at my beck and call the best actors, the best musicians, the best stage hands. So if the play isn't to your liking, do not hesitate to shoot the playwright—but be quick for the curtain is about to rise for Act I.

ACT I

Omar Sharif and the Dallas Aces

Omar Sharif, Ira Corn, Charles and Katherine Wei: these are the names which weave the dominant themes across the pattern of world bridge in the new era.

As the bells rang out the old year and rang in the new for 1970, a spectacular overture ushered in the new age—the age of high stakes, rich prizes and dramatic clashes between colourful personalities.

In the banqueting hall of London's Piccadilly Hotel, converted hastily and at great cost into a theatre and film set, Omar Sharif and his famous Circus fought a rubber bridge duel at £1-a-point against Crockford's Club, championed by Britain's two outstanding players, Jeremy Flint and Jonathan Cansino.

Bridgerama, TV monitors and eight colour cameras, trained on the star-studded audience no less than on the stage, captured every vibrant moment and recorded it for posterity.

Never had bridge been played for such stakes. Never, since the golden age of Culbertson, did an event enjoy so much publicity.

The grand design, conceived by Omar Sharif, was to present bridge as a rich, exciting spectacle; to break through into television and so bring the game within the reach of millions who were still denied its joys.

After the first few rubbers, the Circus took the lead and continued steadily to forge ahead. Omar won £7,000 in stake money. He lost £100,000 on a film which had grave technical faults and was never shown to the public.

Omar Sharif was a good winner. He was an even better loser. Not once have I heard him say a bitter word or blame anyone for what most men, no matter how rich, would have regarded as a catastrophe.

This was the most sensational hand of the entire match.

Dealer North: Game All

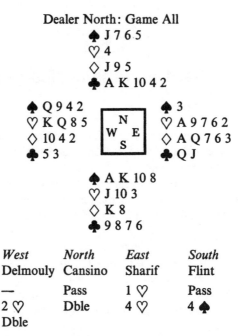

♠ J 7 6 5
♡ 4
◇ J 9 5
♣ A K 10 4 2

♠ Q 9 4 2
♡ K Q 8 5
◇ 10 4 2
♣ 5 3

♠ 3
♡ A 9 7 6 2
◇ A Q 7 6 3
♣ Q J

♠ A K 10 8
♡ J 10 3
◇ K 8
♣ 9 8 7 6

West	North	East	South
Delmouly	*Cansino*	*Sharif*	*Flint*
—	Pass	1 ♡	Pass
2 ♡	Dble	4 ♡	4 ♠
Dble			

Claude Delmouly opened the ♡ K and continued with the ♡ 5. Flint ruffed in dummy and lost the trump finesse to the ♠ Q. A diamond to Omar Sharif's ◇ A and another diamond to the ◇ K followed. After laying down the ♣ A, on which Omar threw the ♣ Q, Flint drew trumps and led a second club.

Should he finesse or play for the drop? Either he would make the contract or he would go four down. Allowing for side bets, some £2,000 hinged on Jeremy's guess. Alas, he finessed and made no more tricks.

Soon after this deal, Giorgio Belladonna, thirteen times champion of the world, gave a good example of his artistry in defence.

Dealer East: Love All

Belladonna

♠ 9 4 3
♡ A J 8
◇ A 10 8 3

Cansino ♣ Q 10 5 Flint

♠ —
♡ 6 5 4 3
◇ 9 6 5 4
♣ 9 8 7 6 3

```
      N
   W     E
      S
```

♠ K Q 10 7 2
♡ Q 10 2
◇ Q 7 2
♣ A K

Garozzo

♠ A J 8 6 5
♡ K 9 7
◇ K J
♣ J 4 2

West	North	East	South
—	—	1 ♠	Pass
Pass	Dble	Pass	Pass
1 NT	Pass	Pass	Dble
Redble	Pass	2 ◇	Dble

Having picked up the worst hand of the match, Cansino did his best to wriggle out of 1 ♠ doubled. Hence the 1 NT, followed by the SOS redouble.

Garozzo opened the ♡ 7 to the ace and Belladonna returned a low trump. Winning with the knave, Garozzo continued with the king. Belladonna took it over with the ◇ A to play a third trump. Flint could now make his ◇ Q. But beware of Italians bearing gifts. They can be more dangerous than the Greeks. Unless Belladonna 'squanders' his ace, declarer ruffs two spades in dummy, instead of one only, and he still scores his ◇ Q by trumping a club.

There was a burst of applause from spectators. Watching on the close-circuit TV monitors, they admired not only Belladonna's technique in overtaking the king of trumps with the ace, but the lightning speed of his play. Brilliance is mere routine for Belladonna.

The play ran much behind schedule and for the last thirty rubbers the duellists retired to Omar's private suite. From a post of vantage, between Giorgio and Jonathan, I was a privileged kibitzer and a guest at the spaghetti supper, with claret for Omar and champagne for the rest of us, which, at five o'clock in the morning, brought proceedings to a close. A few hours later the Circus was on its way to Chicago for a grand tour of seven cities in North America, billed to play a series of matches against the new whiz-kids, the Dallas Aces.

Fought over 844 boards, this marathon introduced a new phase in modern bridge. The Aces 'came of age', as one of them, Billy Eisenberg, was to say later. Though it was a close-run thing, they beat a team which included the world's three greatest players, Giorgio Belladonna, Benito Garozzo, and, in the later stages, Pietro Forquet.

This was, perhaps, the best-played hand of the tour.

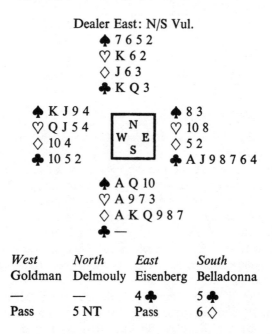

Dealer East: N/S Vul.

```
              ♠ 7 6 5 2
              ♡ K 6 2
              ◇ J 6 3
              ♣ K Q 3
♠ K J 9 4                      ♠ 8 3
♡ Q J 5 4        N             ♡ 10 8
◇ 10 4       W       E         ◇ 5 2
♣ 10 5 2         S             ♣ A J 9 8 7 6 4
              ♠ A Q 10
              ♡ A 9 7 3
              ◇ A K Q 9 8 7
              ♣ —
```

West	North	East	South
Goldman	Delmouly	Eisenberg	Belladonna
—	—	4 ♣	5 ♣
Pass	5 NT	Pass	6 ◇

It was the same contract in both rooms and both Wests led a

club. Again, both declarers went up with dummy's ♣ K, ruffed East's ♣ A and drew trumps. But thereafter their paths differed. For the Aces, Jim Jacoby relied on the spade finesse for his contract and went down.

Belladonna discarded a spade on the ♣ Q, ruffed dummy's third club and ran his trumps to bring about this seven-card ending.

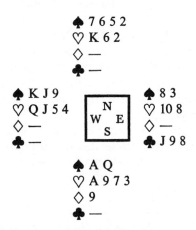

```
              ♠ 7 6 5 2
              ♡ K 6 2
              ◇ —
              ♣ —

  ♠ K J 9                    ♠ 8 3
  ♡ Q J 5 4      N           ♡ 10 8
  ◇ —        W     E         ◇ —
  ♣ —            S           ♣ J 9 8

              ♠ A Q
              ♡ A 9 7 3
              ◇ 9
              ♣ —
```

If, on the last diamond, Goldman, West, threw a heart, Giorgio would play the ♡ A, ♡ K and ♡ 3, setting up a heart and forcing a spade lead into his ♠ A Q. If Goldman parted with a spade, Belladonna would throw a heart from dummy and play the ♠ A and ♠ Q, setting up two spades.

The experience gained by the Aces in what must surely be the longest match in history, the confidence it gave them, the boost to their morale, confirmed them as much the best team in America, and crushing all opposition at home, they went overseas to win two successive world championships. The Bermuda Bowl, symbol of world supremacy, came back to America and the founder of the Aces achieved his ambition.

This brings me to Ira Corn.

Everything about Ira is larger than life—his height, his weight, his house, his Texan conglomerate, and above all, his formidable drive.

Watching the *squadra azzurra* win the New York Olympiad in 1964, Ira Corn made up his mind, there and then, that he would bring back to America the world title which Britain won in 1955 and which had stayed in Europe ever since.

Why were the Italians so good? One reason was that their country was so small, so much smaller than the United States. Living close to each other, Italy's best players could train together and practise all the time. The Americans couldn't. That had to be put right.

Even Ira couldn't bring Los Angeles within easy reach of New York, so he did the next best thing. He picked half a dozen of America's most promising players, brought them to Dallas, provided them with a trainer, a computer, a psychiatrist, and hired them as whole-time professionals to do nothing but play against the best teams in America.

The Aces took part in every major tournament, and when first-class opponents ran short, Ira invited the strongest teams in the country to be his guests in Dallas. If an Ace was missing, Ira took his place.

How good is Ira Corn?

A champion in his own right—he won the National Mixed Pairs with Dorothy Moore—Ira can hold his own in any company.

In *How to Read Opponents' Cards*, Michael Lawrence, one of the original Aces, records this hand played by Ira Corn, shown as West in the diagram.

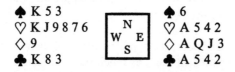

♠ K 5 3   ♠ 6
♡ K J 9 8 7 6   ♡ A 5 4 2
♢ 9   ♢ A Q J 3
♣ K 8 3   ♣ A 5 4 2

After a pass by North, the dealer, East-West bid up to an eminently respectable slam in hearts.

North led the ♣ Q to which South followed with the ♣ 10. A trump to the ♡ A brought the ♡ Q from North. How should Ira Corn continue?

A spade loser is unavoidable, but a club can be discarded on one of dummy's diamonds, so long as the ♢ K is located without loss. Both a straightforward and ruffing finesse are available, but which should it be?

Corn reasoned that North, who had passed as dealer, couldn't have a club suit, the ♠ A and also the ◇ K. But did he have the ♠ A? He daren't play a spade from dummy, for South might ruff a club. So first, South's trump had to be extracted. Back in his hand with the ♡ K, Corn led the ♠ K! When North produced the ♠ A, no problem remained. Ira Corn cashed the ◇ A and led the ◇ Q. Whether or not South covered, Corn's club loser would vanish for evermore.

Not long after the Aces 'came of age' I was featuring hands from Stockholm where they won their first world title in 1970. The Chinese from Taiwan were their most dangerous opponents.

A system bid led to a curious result on this deal. The Aces sat North-South.

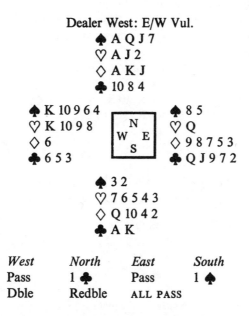

Dealer West: E/W Vul.

```
          ♠ A Q J 7
          ♡ A J 2
          ◇ A K J
          ♣ 10 8 4

♠ K 10 9 6 4        N        ♠ 8 5
♡ K 10 9 8       W     E     ♡ Q
◇ 6                 S        ◇ 9 8 7 5 3
♣ 6 5 3                      ♣ Q J 9 7 2

          ♠ 3 2
          ♡ 7 6 5 4 3
          ◇ Q 10 4 2
          ♣ A K
```

West	North	East	South
Pass	1 ♣	Pass	1 ♠
Dble	Redble	ALL PASS	

South's 1 ♠ response showed three controls—an ace and a king or three kings. It had no bearing on the spade suit. The Chinese West doubled to suggest a lead, little thinking that the bidding would stop. Bobby Wolff, North, thought otherwise, and when he re-doubled, Jim Jacoby, South, with two spades more than he had promised, passed happily.

West led his ◇ 6 and Jacoby returned the suit, forcing him to ruff. Coming in with the ♡ A, he forced West again, ending with nine tricks—a diamond, a heart, two clubs, a club ruff and dummy's four spades.

It is tempting to double an artificial bid, but there are times when even temptation must be resisted. One of them is when the doubler cannot stand a redouble.

Admittedly, with Italy represented by a team of 'tourists' and neither France nor Britain in the field, the opposition in Stockholm was only moderate. It was much stiffer the following year in Taipeh when the Aces overwhelmed another American formation, as well as Australia, Taiwan and Brazil, before defeating a very strong French team, in the finals.

Many experts look on Bobby Wolff as the ace of Aces. This was one of his brilliant performances at Taipeh.

Dealer East: Love All

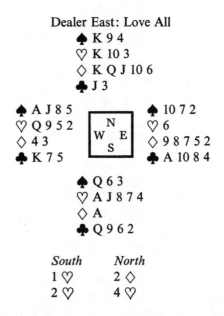

```
                      ♠ K 9 4
                      ♡ K 10 3
                      ◇ K Q J 10 6
                      ♣ J 3
      ♠ A J 8 5                       ♠ 10 7 2
      ♡ Q 9 5 2        N              ♡ 6
      ◇ 4 3         W     E           ◇ 9 8 7 5 2
      ♣ K 7 5          S              ♣ A 10 8 4
                      ♠ Q 6 3
                      ♡ A J 8 7 4
                      ◇ A
                      ♣ Q 9 6 2
```

South	North
1 ♡	2 ◇
2 ♡	4 ♡

Svarc, the French West, led the ♣ 5 to Boulenger's ♣ A. The
♠ 2 came back. Winning with the ♠ A, Svarc cashed the ♣ K
and exited with a spade to Wolff's ♠ Q. Without seeing all four
hands, how can declarer avoid the loss of a trump trick?

Bobby Wolff peered into Svarc's mind and found the answer.
Why had Svarc been so anxious to cash his winners? It seemed
rather rash—unless, of course, he felt confident that he would
take one more trick to set the contract. That trick could only be
the ♡ Q. By itself the queen offered only a fifty-fifty chance, so
Bobby placed Svarc with Q 9 x x, his actual holding. At trick five
he led the ♡ J, covered, in turn, by the ♡ Q and ♡ K. Coming to
his hand with the ◇ A, he ran the ♡ 8 and so brought home a
seemingly impossible contract.

Here is Bob Hamman, sitting East.

Dealer South: Game All

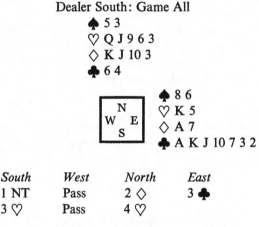

    ♠ 5 3
    ♡ Q J 9 6 3
    ◇ K J 10 3
    ♣ 6 4

                      ♠ 8 6
                      ♡ K 5
                      ◇ A 7
                      ♣ A K J 10 7 3 2

South	West	North	East
1 NT	Pass	2 ◇	3 ♣
3 ♡	Pass	4 ♡	

South's 1 NT promised 16–18 and North's 2 ◇ was a transfer
bid, calling for a rebid in hearts. The jump to 3 ♡ was encourag-
ing, but did not guarantee four trumps.

West led the ♣ 9.

Putting yourself in East's place, how would you set about
defeating the contract?

It was clear to Hamman that West could contribute nothing.
So he devised a neat swindle. After taking the ♣ A K, he cashed
the ◇ A—just as if it were a singleton—and continued with the

♠ 6! Ostensibly, he was trying to put West in to get a diamond ruff. These were the other hands.

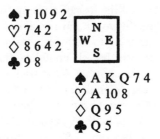

♠ J 10 9 2
♡ 7 4 2
♢ 8 6 4 2
♣ 9 8

♠ A K Q 7 4
♡ A 10 8
♢ Q 9 5
♣ Q 5

Falling into the trap and needing the heart finesse, declarer cashed a second spade and tried to reach dummy by ruffing a third spade. Bob Hamman promptly over-ruffed. A subtle defence, and the ♠ 6 was a subtle card.

Like Omar Sharif, Ira Corn has always planned to break into TV. Sponsored by Hallmark, the greeting cards manufacturers, a film with a new technique was presented to viewers shortly after Taipeh. Unheard by the others, every player in turn spoke his thoughts aloud, making it possible for the audience to follow the reasoning behind every move.

The match was between Ira Corn's Aces and a team captained by Charles Goren. This was one of the swings to the Aces.

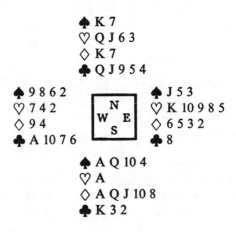

♠ K 7
♡ Q J 6 3
♢ K 7
♣ Q J 9 5 4

♠ 9 8 6 2
♡ 7 4 2
♢ 9 4
♣ A 10 7 6

♠ J 5 3
♡ K 10 9 8 5
♢ 6 5 3 2
♣ 8

♠ A Q 10 4
♡ A
♢ A Q J 10 8
♣ K 3 2

The Goren team stopped in 3 NT, scoring 660. For the Aces, Billy Eisenberg and Bob Hamman, playing the Blue Club, reached 6 ♣ with Eisenberg, South, as declarer. In view of the bad trump break, the play required careful timing.

A heart to the ♡ A was followed by a trump to dummy's queen and another to South's king and West's ace. A second heart removed South's last trump. To catch the guarded ♣ 10, Eisenberg first shortened dummy's trumps by ruffing a master diamond. Then he played out his winners. In the two-card ending, West was forced to ruff in front of dummy.

The film's rating was poor, surprisingly so, for the Aces were riding on the crest of a wave and it was an ideal moment to exploit their prestige and their popularity.

FIRST INTERVAL
Cavalcade
the bridge scene shifts from day to day

Taipeh was the last scene in the First Act of the struggle for world supremacy. During the interval, while a hundred stage hands, each one a star, change the scenery, and set the props for Act II, we shall watch the fast-moving cavalcade of tournaments, national and international, which make up the annual bridge calendar.

The canvas will be smaller than in Stockholm or Taipeh, the prizes will lack the prestige of the Bermuda Bowl, but the drama and suspense, the hopes and fears of those taking part, will be no less real and just as tense.

Even before Omar Sharif's Circus was airborne on the way to Chicago, invitations were going out from the British Bridge League for the *Sunday Times* Tournament, one of the most exclusive pairs events in the world.

The weak NT (12–14) had a marked success on this *Sunday Times* hand.

Dealer East: N/S Vul.
♠ K J 6
♡ Q 8 4
◇ A 10 8 6
♣ A 10 3

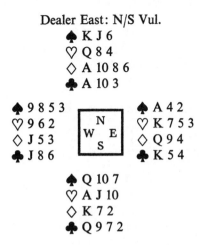

♠ 9 8 5 3   ♠ A 4 2
♡ 9 6 2   ♡ K 7 5 3
◇ J 5 3   ◇ Q 9 4
♣ J 8 6   ♣ K 5 4

♠ Q 10 7
♡ A J 10
◇ K 7 2
♣ Q 9 7 2

Most North-South pairs were in 3 NT, scoring 630. At two tables, however, the weak 1 NT jockeyed them out of game. When Joel Tarlo, East, opened 1 NT, Boris Schapiro, West, bid 2 ♠ on his near-Yarborough and hoped for the best. It happened. Their strength being divided, opponents did not like to intervene and Schapiro went four down peacefully, stopping a vulnerable game for 200.

Nico Gardener had the same idea as Schapiro. When Tony Priday, his partner, bid 1 NT, Gardener brazenly called 2 ♣, the Stayman convention, asking for a four-card major. Priday replied 2 ♡, held the bid and made four tricks. Again it cost 200 to stop 630.

Admittedly, the weak no trump can be dangerous, but it makes life dangerous for opponents too, and not a few of our leading players use it regardless of vulnerability.

Gardener and Priday went on to win. Here they are again next year, opposing America's Jordan and Robinson, who are West and East in the diagram.

Dealer East: Love All

♠ A K J 9
♡ J
◇ A 10 9 6
♣ K 9 4 3

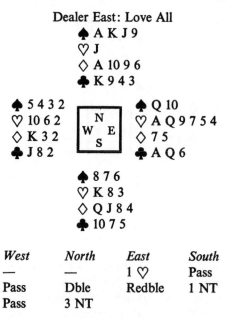

♠ 5 4 3 2
♡ 10 6 2
◇ K 3 2
♣ J 8 2

♠ Q 10
♡ A Q 9 7 5 4
◇ 7 5
♣ A Q 6

♠ 8 7 6
♡ K 8 3
◇ Q J 8 4
♣ 10 7 5

West	North	East	South
—	—	1 ♡	Pass
Pass	Dble	Redble	1 NT
Pass	3 NT		

Gardener, North, expected more from Priday's free bid of
1 NT. Priday, for his part, found himself between Scylla and
Charybdis, too good to pass and too bad to bid. The latter
appeared to him to be the lesser evil.

Jordan opened a heart to Robinson's ♡ A. Priday ducked a
second heart, won the third and took the diamond finesse. When
it succeeded, he could see seven tricks. What next?

The average player would take the spade finesse and blame
partner for bidding 3 NT—or defend himself for bidding 1 NT.
Tony Priday did neither. Since Jordan, who had passed his
partner's 1 ♡, had produced the ◇ K, he was unlikely to have
the ♠ Q as well. So Priday laid down the ♠ A K, dropping the
♠ Q and ♠ 10, and claimed nine tricks. A lucky hand on which
good play made up for a dubious bid.

The winners this time were Bob Slavenburg, playing with Leon
Tintner. They had a neck and neck race with Omar Sharif and
Benito Garozzo, who came second. Kibitzers crowded round the
table when the two pairs met. This was the critical board.

Dealer West: Love All

♠ —
♡ Q 7 6 5
◇ K Q 10 8 5 2
♣ Q J 7

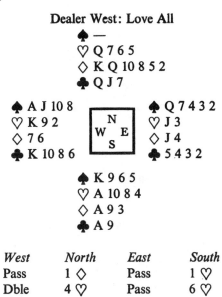

♠ A J 10 8
♡ K 9 2
◇ 7 6
♣ K 10 8 6

♠ Q 7 4 3 2
♡ J 3
◇ J 4
♣ 5 4 3 2

♠ K 9 6 5
♡ A 10 8 4
◇ A 9 3
♣ A 9

West	North	East	South
Pass	1 ◇	Pass	1 ♡
Dble	4 ♡	Pass	6 ♡

Slavenburg, South, was somewhat startled to see his dummy. He had expected partner to have a little more—or a lot more—for his jump to 4 ♡.

Garozzo, West, led the ♠ A, which Slavenburg ruffed in dummy. How should he continue? He had to lead trumps from the table, for if he crossed to his hand with a diamond, a diamond might later be ruffed.

Since Garozzo, who came in with a second round double, had passed as dealer, his hand was clearly distributional. He might have one heart honour, but Omar could have both. So at trick two, Bob Slavenburg led the ♡ Q and ran it. Garozzo played low, but when Omar Sharif followed to the next trick with the ♡ J, Bob could spread his hand.

January is a busy month for bridge. If the *Sunday Times* Pairs is the most exclusive event in terms of expertise, the most exclusive socially is the St. Moritz tournament held in four of the most luxurious hotels in Europe. Among London players who take part regularly is George Lengyel, former Dutch international, now a regular at the Eccentric Club in London. Here is Lengyel in action.

Dealer West: Love All

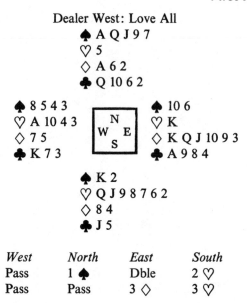

♠ A Q J 9 7
♡ 5
◇ A 6 2
♣ Q 10 6 2

♠ 8 5 4 3   ♠ 10 6
♡ A 10 4 3   ♡ K
◇ 7 5   ◇ K Q J 10 9 3
♣ K 7 3   ♣ A 9 8 4

♠ K 2
♡ Q J 9 8 7 6 2
◇ 8 4
♣ J 5

West	North	East	South
Pass	1 ♠	Dble	2 ♡
Pass	Pass	3 ◇	3 ♡

West led the ◇ 7 and six possible losers came into view—a diamond, two clubs, and three trumps. Lengyel, South, went up with the ◇ A and continued with three top spades. East ruffed with his ♡ K and Lengyel shed the ◇ 8. Next came the ◇ K, and thinking ahead, declarer ruffed with the ♡ 6.

Now came the lowly ♡ 2. With only the ♡ 5 on view West wouldn't waste an honour, and suddenly a precious entry appeared in dummy. A club was parked on the ♠ J and another on the ♠ 9. West ruffed and scored his ♡ A. Lengyel didn't try to talk him out of it.

In February, the spotlight is on the Royal Bridge Festival in Tangier. Golf in the morning and champagne parties in the evening make every lively day a social occasion. This in no way detracts from the bridge.

Here are Tony Priday and Claude Rodrigue, runners-up in 1975.

Dealer West: Both Vul.

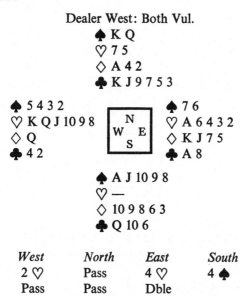

♠ K Q
♡ 7 5
◇ A 4 2
♣ K J 9 7 5 3

♠ 5 4 3 2
♡ K Q J 10 9 8
◇ Q
♣ 4 2

♠ 7 6
♡ A 6 4 3 2
◇ K J 7 5
♣ A 8

♠ A J 10 9 8
♡ —
◇ 10 9 8 6 3
♣ Q 10 6

West	North	East	South
2 ♡	Pass	4 ♡	4 ♠
Pass	Pass	Dble	

West's 2 ♡ was, of course, the Weak Two type. Had North bid 3 ♣, it would have been conventional, asking South to bid. So Priday passed.

Playing for money or in a teams event, Rodrigue, South, would have doubtless passed 4 ♡. With match-point scoring, things are different. All bottoms are equally cold, but if a gamble comes off the reward may be a rich one. Hence the audacious 4 ♠.

West led the ♡ K, ruffed by South. If he now draws trumps, he is undone, for he must lose the lead to the ♣ A and he cannot afford to be forced again. So, at trick two, Rodrigue led a club. East won and persisted with hearts, but Claude simply discarded a diamond. The next heart could be ruffed in dummy.

A dramatic setting adds interest to the best of hands—even if it owes something to the imagination—so while we are in Tangier we should recall a hand entitled the *Morocco Coup*, which is said to have been played in King Hassan's palace during an attempt to assassinate him.

The bidding isn't known, but the contract was 6 ♠.

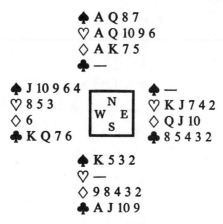

West made the obvious lead, the ♣ K. Leaving out of account a bomb explosion while the game was in progress, can the contract be made?

This is what happened.

Discarding a diamond from dummy, declarer went up with the ♣ A and played the ♣ J, covered and ruffed. After the ♡ A and a heart ruff, South cashed his two winning clubs, throwing the ◇ 7 and ◇ K from dummy and led a trump. West played the ♠ 9, and dummy's ♠ Q won. After a heart ruff, declarer crossed to the ◇ A and ruffed another heart with the ♠ K, West having to under-ruff. In the three-card ending, West remained with ♠ J 10 6 under dummy's ♠ A 8 ♡ Q.

South led a diamond, and West could only score one trick. In the event, he ruffed with the ♠ 10, and South discarded dummy's ♡ Q.

Many visitors, especially from the United States are attracted to the annual Bridge Festival in Israel. This hand is from the first International Congress held in Tel Aviv in 1966. South was world champion Rixi Markus. East was the German international, Egmont von Dewitz.

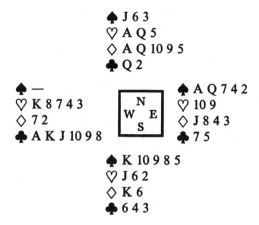

♠ J 6 3
♡ A Q 5
◇ A Q 10 9 5
♣ Q 2

♠ —
♡ K 8 7 4 3
◇ 7 2
♣ A K J 10 9 8

♠ A Q 7 4 2
♡ 10 9
◇ J 8 4 3
♣ 7 5

♠ K 10 9 8 5
♡ J 6 2
◇ K 6
♣ 6 4 3

After a spirited auction, Rixi Markus, South, found herself in
4 ♠, doubled by von Dewitz. West started with the ♣ A K, but
despite partner's encouragement, switched to a diamond. The
◇ 10, ◇ J and ◇ K made up the trick.

Rixi negotiated the heart finesse and led the ♠ J, ducked by
von Dewitz. A second trump to the ♠ 10 in the closed hand
followed.

The red aces provided two vital entries to dummy, first to lead
the third trump, then to cash the diamonds, setting the stage for a
trump coup. Von Dewitz went up with the ♠ A on the third
trump, but when she led dummy's last diamond, Rixi Markus
still had the ♠ K 10 poised over his Q 7.

The story went round Tel Aviv at the time that Egmont had
offered a cup to the most successful German competitor. That he
was his country's only representative was, of course, a mere
coincidence.

In Britain, the spring season is crowded with events which
often overlap. The first is the English Bridge Union's Spring
Foursomes held at Eastbourne.

The following hand features Nicola Gardener, for long our
youngest Life Master.

Her birthday was a good occasion to recall this hand which,
while still a teenager, she played at the Spring Foursomes of 1969.
North was her father, Nico, three times European champion.

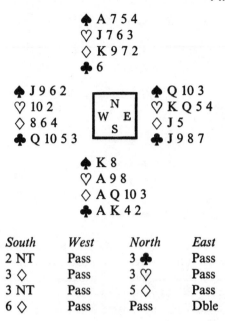

♠ A 7 5 4
♡ J 7 6 3
◇ K 9 7 2
♣ 6

♠ J 9 6 2
♡ 10 2
◇ 8 6 4
♣ Q 10 5 3

♠ Q 10 3
♡ K Q 5 4
◇ J 5
♣ J 9 8 7

♠ K 8
♡ A 9 8
◇ A Q 10 3
♣ A K 4 2

South	West	North	East
2 NT	Pass	3 ♣	Pass
3 ◇	Pass	3 ♡	Pass
3 NT	Pass	5 ◇	Pass
6 ◇	Pass	Pass	Dble

Nico Gardener's 3 ♣ was conventional. Having found the 4–4 diamond fit, Nicola, a forward young lady, shot the slam.

She won the trump lead in her hand, laid down the top clubs and ruffed the other two in dummy, drawing trumps in the process. Two spades and a spade ruff left East with hearts only. Remembering his double, Nicola led the ♡ 9 and ran it. East won with the ♡ K, but then had to lead away from the ♡ Q, presenting Nicola with her twelfth trick.

The word 'squeeze' is apt to bemuse all but the best players and many squeezes, it is true, are difficult. Some are quite simple and a few materialize on their own—well, almost on their own. Here is an example from the Master Pairs, another spring event.

♠ K Q 10 8 7 6 5 2
♡ —
◇ 4 3
♣ K 5 4

♠ 9
♡ 5 4 3 2
◇ K J 10 5
♣ Q 8 7 6

♠ 4 3
♡ K Q 8 7 6
◇ 9 8 7 6
♣ J 9

♠ A J
♡ A J 10 9
◇ A Q 2
♣ A 10 3 2

Several pairs reached 7 ♠ and all but one went down. Derek Rimington and Bob Rowlands were in 7 NT.

The ♠ 9 was led to the ♠ A and Rimington could see twelve tricks only. He tried the ♣ K and ♣ A, in case the ♣ Q J were alone. Then he cashed the ♡ A and set about the spades. Discarding on an eight-card suit is a nightmare and in trying to guide partner one may easily help declarer. So it was here. Early on, East threw the ♡ K, telling West not to worry about hearts. Now, when at last he came to the eighth spade and East still had the ♡ Q, Derek could shed his ♡ J, retaining the ◇ A Q, as his last two cards. Should he finesse? No question. When East played the ◇ 9, his other card was known to be the ♡ Q. West had to keep a club, so the ◇ K dropped on the ◇ A, as Derek knew it would.

The next four hands are from the *Guardian* Easter Tournament. On the first, the French international, Leon Tintner, sat West. East was Louis Tarlo.

Dealer West: Game All

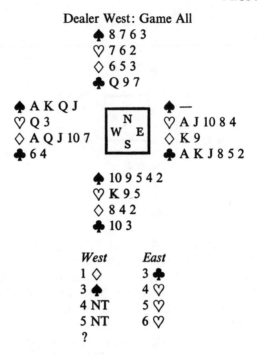

West	East
1 ◊	3 ♣
3 ♠	4 ♡
4 NT	5 ♡
5 NT	6 ♡
?	

With a preview of East's hand, West's bid would be 7 ◊. Even on a heart lead, life is rosy. The ♡ A goes up, four hearts are thrown on the spades and a heart ruff yields the thirteenth trick.

At rubber bridge 7 ◊ would be the ideal contract. Not so at match-pointed pairs, where everyone holds the same cards. Looking for a top—a better score than that of any other East-West pair—Leon Tintner bid 7 NT. The ♡ 2 was an unfriendly lead, especially as North, Nico Gardener, was just the man to lead away from the ♡ K.

Tintner went up with the ♡ A and later took the club finesse.

A shocking grand slam at rubber bridge. A well-judged gamble at match-points—especially as it came off.

Here's another example of the difference imposed by match-point scoring between duplicate pairs and rubber bridge. Omar Sharif was South. North was Boris Schapiro.

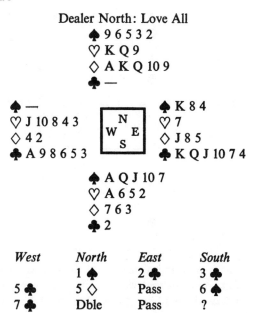

Dealer North: Love All

```
           ♠ 9 6 5 3 2
           ♡ K Q 9
           ◇ A K Q 10 9
           ♣ —

♠ —                        ♠ K 8 4
♡ J 10 8 4 3      N        ♡ 7
◇ 4 2          W     E     ◇ J 8 5
♣ A 9 8 6 5 3     S        ♣ K Q J 10 7 4

           ♠ A Q J 10 7
           ♡ A 6 5 2
           ◇ 7 6 3
           ♣ 2
```

West	North	East	South
	1 ♠	2 ♣	3 ♣
5 ♣	5 ◇	Pass	6 ♠
7 ♣	Dble	Pass	?

In the discussion which followed before the VuGraph screen, Omar Sharif maintained that he should have bid 7 ♠.

Boris Schapiro's double was a warning. Having opened on a suite, headed by the nine, he couldn't make a forcing pass, inviting a grand slam. But Omar knew that 7 ♠ would probably depend on a finesse. At rubber bridge, a grand slam on a finesse is a crime. In a pairs event it may be the right thing to do. Few East-Wests will sacrifice in 7 ♣, so North-South at this table have been unlucky. Going down in 7 ♠ will only be a little worse than collecting 500 or 700 or 900. But if the grand slam succeeds, as it would do here, a near-bottom will look very much like a top.

There's much truth in the ancient Chinese dictum that however hard a blow may be, it might conceivably be harder.

Dealer South: E/W Game

```
              ♠ —
              ♡ J 6
              ◇ J 10 9 2
              ♣ 10 9 7 6 5 4 2

♠ Q 10 7 6 4                    ♠ A K J 9 8 5
♡ 5 4           N              ♡ K 3 2
◇ 8 7 6 5 3   W   E            ◇ A K Q
♣ 3             S              ♣ J

              ♠ 3 2
              ♡ A Q 10 9 8 7
              ◇ 4
              ♣ A K Q 8
```

South opened 1 ♡ and two passes followed. Some Easts now bid 2 ♡. Others preferred a jump to 4 ♠. But whatever he did, every East felt confident that with his rock-crusher, he had right of way. This was the bidding at the table where I sat East.

South	*West*	*North*	*East*
1 ♡	Pass	Pass	2 ♡
3 ♣	Pass	Pass	4 ♠
Pass	Pass	5 ♣	Pass
Pass	5 ♠	Pass	Pass
Dble	Pass	6 ♣	Dble

Opponents had been willing to play in 1 ♡ and again in 3 ♣, so I was expecting a tidy penalty. A diamond was opened to my ◇ A. Then South wrapped up twelve tricks. Surely, I thought, a catastrophic result. I unfolded the score-sheet and I was heartened to see that still greater misfortunes had befallen my neighbours. Two other pairs were in 6 ♣ and on a spade lead made all thirteen tricks. And one of the visiting pairs from Germany, Prince Zu Waldeck and Fritz Chodziesner, who won the tournament, had been driven into 7 ♣. Again a spade was led and their gallant sacrifice turned into a happily fulfilled grand slam.

Dealer West: N/S Game

♠ J 10 6
♡ A J 2
◇ Q 8 7
♣ A K J 6

♠ Q 7 3   ♠ A K 8 5
♡ K Q 7 5   ♡ 6 4
◇ A 9 3   ◇ K J 5 4
♣ Q 5 4   ♣ 10 7 2

♠ 9 4 2
♡ 10 9 8 3
◇ 10 6 2
♣ 9 8 3

You are East. Partner opens 1 NT, showing 12–14 points, and
North doubles. This is a situation made for the weak no-trump
and you redouble promptly, knowing that you have the balance of
strength. You are ready, willing and able to double opponents if
they seek refuge in any one of three suits, leaving partner to look
after the fourth. The redouble is left in, however, and partner
proceeds to make nine tricks, four spades, four diamonds and a
heart.

This innocent part-score hand—for you were going to pass
1 NT—has brought you 910 points. Surely, you say, it must be a
cold, undisputed top. Then you open the travelling score-sheet
and discover that precisely the same thing has happened at three
other tables. And at two more; North-South, trying to wriggle
out of the redouble, were set 1,100 in 2 ♣ and likewise in 2 ♡
doubled.

Almost every West had opened 1 NT. Terence Reese was
probably the only North to pass. For the others, who doubled, it
became a question of staying in the frying-pan or jumping
smartly into the fire.

If bridge maturity is a pointer to manhood, it may not be long
before the fifteen- and sixteen-year-olds demand the vote. That
was one of the lessons of the finals of the *Daily Mail* Cup for
Schools in 1970, won by the Royal Grammar School, Newcastle-

on-Tyne. This was a big and well-deserved swing for the winners.

```
                    ♠ 10
                    ♡ A Q J 8 4 3
                    ◇ A K 6
                    ♣ A K J

♠ K J 9 7 6 5              ♠ A Q 8 4 3
♡ 9            ┌───────┐   ♡ K 7 6 5 2
◇ 10 4 3 2     │   N   │   ◇ Q 7
♣ 8 4         │ W   E │   ♣ 2
               │   S   │
               └───────┘
                    ♠ 2
                    ♡ 10
                    ◇ J 9 8 5
                    ♣ Q 10 9 7 6 5 3
```

With the Royal Grammar School sitting East-West, the bidding was:

West	North	East	South
3 ♠	3 NT	4 ♠	Pass
Pass	5 ♡	Pass!	—

Warned by partner's pre-emptive opening, East wisely refrained from doubling. He was glad to accept 100.

Turn to the other room.

West	North	East	South
Pass	2 ♡	Pass	2 NT
Pass	4 ♡	Dble	5 ♣
Pass	6 ♣!		

North reasoned that even with two hearts, South would not have rescued. And if he had one or none, he would be able to set up a long heart in dummy after taking a ruffing finesse against West, who must surely have the ♡ K for his double. And that is exactly what happened.

The spotlight is still on youth, but two years have elapsed and the occasion is the Junior European Championship. Sitting South is Germany's Splettösser, aged fifteen.

Dealer South: Both Vul.

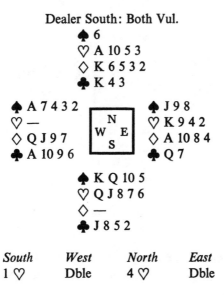

	♠ 6	
	♡ A 10 5 3	
	◊ K 6 5 3 2	
	♣ K 4 3	

♠ A 7 4 3 2　　　　　　　♠ J 9 8
♡ —　　　　　　　　　　♡ K 9 4 2
◊ Q J 9 7　　　　　　　◊ A 10 8 4
♣ A 10 9 6　　　　　　♣ Q 7

	♠ K Q 10 5	
	♡ Q J 8 7 6	
	◊ —	
	♣ J 8 5 2	

South	*West*	*North*	*East*
1 ♡	Dble	4 ♡	Dble

The 1 ♡ opening was, perhaps, a trifle foolhardy. The play, aided by a slip in defence, more than made up for it.

West opened the ♠ A and switched to the ◊ Q. South ruffed, crossed to the ♡ A, bringing to light the 4–0 trump break, and ruffed a second diamond.

Next came the ♣ J, a cunning move which caught West nodding. When he played low, South rose with the ♣ K and ruffed another diamond. Dummy's two remaining clubs now disappeared on the ♠ K Q, and after ruffing a club in dummy and a fourth diamond in his hand, South exited with the ♠ 10, discarding dummy's last diamond.

East ruffed, but with trumps only left, he had to lead one from his K 9 up to dummy's 10 5.

Another two years elapse and we have the 1975 Gold Cup carried off by David Greenwood with much the youngest team ever to win Britain's premier tournament.

David was South on this deal from the finals.

Dealer West: Love All

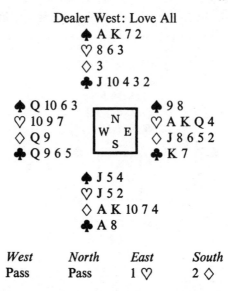

West	North	East	South
Pass	Pass	1 ♡	2 ◇

With a singleton in dummy and trumps breaking 5–2, the contract looks singularly unpromising. Greenwood brought it home just the same.

West led the ♡ 10. After cashing the ♡ A K Q, East continued with a fourth heart. Greenwood shed his ♣ 8 and West ruffed. The sight of the ◇ 9 alerted David Greenwood to the likelihood of a bad trump break and he played accordingly.

Coming in at trick five with the ♣ A, he crossed to the ♠ A and ruffed a club. Back to dummy with the ♠ K, he led another club. With trumps only left, East had to ruff. David over-ruffed, laid down the ◇ A, bringing down West's ◇ Q, and exited with a spade. East couldn't avoid ruffing his partner's trick and leading away from his ◇ J.

With a little help from the opposition, David Greenwood came to eight tricks, scoring all his five trumps, the ♣ A and the ♠ A K.

As April gets under way, the bridge columnist looks for material to the Camrose Cup, the home international.

A spectacular hand from the 1970 match between victorious Scotland and Northern Ireland is a good example of the purist's mentality.

♠ Q 5 2
♡ K J 7 6
◇ J 10 7
♣ A Q 6

♠ 4 3　　　　　　　　　　♠ J 8
♡ Q 10 8 3　　　　　　　♡ 9 5 4 2
◇ 9 6 4 3　　　　　　　◇ K 8 2
♣ 8 5 4　　　　　　　　♣ J 10 7 2

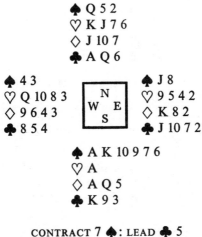

♠ A K 10 9 7 6
♡ A
◇ A Q 5
♣ K 9 3

CONTRACT 7 ♠ : LEAD ♣ 5

Declarer was Gold Cup winner, H. W. Kelsey, author of several books on advanced play. He says: 'I went down in a grand slam which any beginner would have made, but I believe the odds were on my side.'

The beginner takes the diamond finesse. The better player tries to bring down the ♡ Q, then finesses the diamond. The expert sees another chance. He cashes eleven winners, retaining the ♡ J and a diamond in dummy, and the ◇ A Q in his hand. He can still finesse, but he may play West for both the ◇ K and the ♡ Q. If so, the ◇ K, now bare, will fall on the ◇ A.

That is how Kelsey played it. He reasoned that had East the ◇ K, West might have opened a diamond or a club, but if West had the ◇ K, he couldn't lead the suit. His choice would therefore be restricted. So, since West had led a club, he was more likely than East to have the ◇ K, which made the squeeze preferable to the finesse. An unlucky board—but only for an expert. And over a period the expert will win anyway.

Irving Rose, playing for England against Scotland, is declarer here:

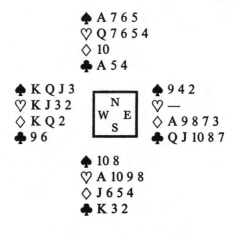

♠ A 7 6 5
♡ Q 7 6 5 4
♢ 10
♣ A 5 4

♠ K Q J 3
♡ K J 3 2
♢ K Q 2
♣ 9 6

♠ 9 4 2
♡ —
♢ A 9 8 7 3
♣ Q J 10 8 7

♠ 10 8
♡ A 10 9 8
♢ J 6 5 4
♣ K 3 2

CONTRACT 4 ♡ DOUBLED

What will be the result? A knowledgeable England supporter assessed the damage at 500 and quickly left the room.

West led a trump and, coming in with a diamond at trick two, a second trump. Rose, South, won in his hand and ducked a spade to West, who returned another spade. Having lost two tricks, Irving Rose still had a trump and a club to lose. Now watch the vanishing trick.

Going up with the ♠ A, Rose ruffed a spade, ruffed a diamond, and after cashing the ♣ K and ♣ A, ruffed dummy's last spade with the ♡ A. Now came the fourth diamond, the *coup de grâce*. West's last two cards were the ♡ K J and in no way could he prevent the ♡ Q poised over him from scoring declarer's tenth trick.

A third trump from West, when he is in with a spade, costs a trump trick but beats the contract.

Almost every deal could be described as dramatic in the cliff-hanger between England and Scotland for the 1975 Camrose Cup, which England won by a single Victory Point. Even had the margin been less desperately narrow, this deal might have proved decisive.

Dealer East: N/S Vul.

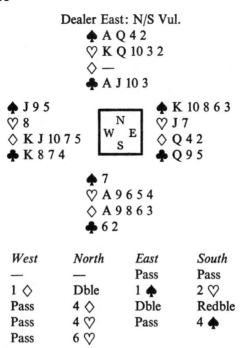

♠ A Q 4 2
♡ K Q 10 3 2
◇ —
♣ A J 10 3

♠ J 9 5
♡ 8
◇ K J 10 7 5
♣ K 8 7 4

♠ K 10 8 6 3
♡ J 7
◇ Q 4 2
♣ Q 9 5

♠ 7
♡ A 9 6 5 4
◇ A 9 8 6 3
♣ 6 2

West	North	East	South
—	—	Pass	Pass
1 ◇	Dble	1 ♠	2 ♡
Pass	4 ◇	Dble	Redble
Pass	4 ♡	Pass	4 ♠
Pass	6 ♡		

South was Claude Rodrigue and North was Tony Priday. Tony's jump to 4 ◇ showed a void and invited a slam. Claude's redouble indicated the ◇ A and accepted the invitation.

A diamond was led. How should South play?

Fearing an over-ruff in diamonds, Rodrigue dare not attempt a complete cross-ruff, while if he drew trumps he would end up a trick short.

In view of West's opening bid, should he take the spade finesse? Luckily for England, Claude Rodrigue found a far better chance —two finesses in clubs. That ensured the contract if the honours were split, if West had both or if the ♠ K came down after two ruffs.

A regular spring event is the Charity Challenge Cup. At the hub of the administration is the indefatigable Jill Gatti.

Some thirty hands, chosen by experts, mainly from past tournaments, are pre-dealt and played simultaneously throughout the world.

As might be expected, the results are infinitely varied, but each competitor sees the records and can measure his skill against that of the player who first held the hand.

An amusing example goes back to the Thailand-Lebanon encounter in the 1968 Olympiad, selected for the Charity Cup by Jack Marx.

In one room, the Thai West opened 4 ♡, East raised to 6 ♡, and on the inevitable diamond lead, the slam went one down. Had it been South's lead, it might well have been made.

In the other room, events took a dramatic turn.

Dealer West: E/W Vul.

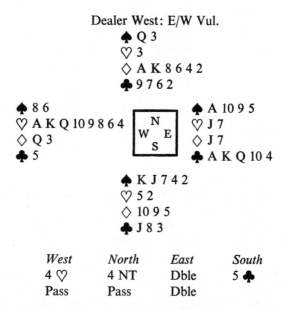

```
                    ♠ Q 3
                    ♡ 3
                    ◇ A K 8 6 4 2
                    ♣ 9 7 6 2
  ♠ 8 6                            ♠ A 10 9 5
  ♡ A K Q 10 9 8 6 4      N        ♡ J 7
  ◇ Q 3                 W   E       ◇ J 7
  ♣ 5                     S         ♣ A K Q 10 4
                    ♠ K J 7 4 2
                    ♡ 5 2
                    ◇ 10 9 5
                    ♣ J 8 3
```

West	North	East	South
4 ♡	4 NT	Dble	5 ♣
Pass	Pass	Dble	

North's 4 NT was the 'unusual' type, asking for partner's longer minor. South, who might have passed to proclaim an unhappy neutrality, made the wrong choice, and on a trump lead made not a single trick. The Thai score sheet read: 5 ♣ Doubled: minus 11: —2,100.

Another charity event, killed by the ill-conceived Gaming Act, was the Faber Cup, the Rubber Bridge Competition organized in aid of Action for the Crippled Child.

The next two hands go back to 1969, the last year in which the competition was held. On both, tactics are paramount.

At Game All, in the sixth and final rubber, East-West were a thousand points down. So if they took the rubber at this score, they would be knocked out of the competition on aggregate.

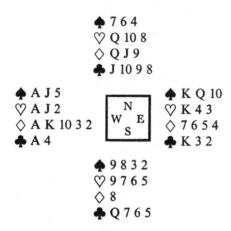

♠ 7 6 4
♡ Q 10 8
◇ Q J 9
♣ J 10 9 8

♠ A J 5   ♠ K Q 10
♡ A J 2   ♡ K 4 3
◇ A K 10 3 2 ◇ 7 6 5 4
♣ A 4   ♣ K 3 2

♠ 9 8 3 2
♡ 9 7 6 5
◇ 8
♣ Q 7 6 5

West dealt and opened 2 NT, expecting partner to pass unless he saw a slam. Unthinkingly, East raised to 3 NT. What could poor West do to avoid winning the rubber and losing the match? He found an ingenious solution—4 ◇, giving partner a second chance to pass under game level. East now saw the light, but he saw something else too, a chance to win the rubber without losing the match for, if West had a diamond suit, the slam couldn't be far off. But this was no time for half-measures. There was no room for any delicate cue-bid. East had to take the plunge himself and he boldly bid 6 ◇.

With the 3–1 trump break and the ♡ Q offside, it looks like an unlucky contract. West made it by simple elimination. He laid down the ◇ A K, ruffed dummy's third club, cashed the spades and exited with a trump. North had to concede a ruff and discard or lead away from his ♡ Q.

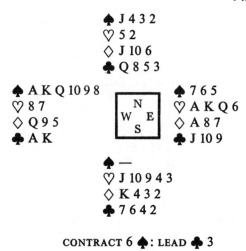

♠ J 4 3 2
♡ 5 2
◇ J 10 6
♣ Q 8 5 3

♠ A K Q 10 9 8
♡ 8 7
◇ Q 9 5
♣ A K

♠ 7 6 5
♡ A K Q 6
◇ A 8 7
♣ J 10 9

♠ —
♡ J 10 9 4 3
◇ K 4 3 2
♣ 7 6 4 2

CONTRACT 6 ♠: LEAD ♣ 3

On the last hand West's problem was to avoid winning the rubber unless his side, 1,000 down on aggregate, could make a slam. This time, opponents were only 300 ahead when, at Game All, with a part-score of 70, East dealt and bid 1 ♡. To win the six-rubber match, West had only to pass or to call a modest 1 ♠. The lure of the slam proved irresistible and with the aid of Blackwood he went on to 6 ♠. An hour later, opponents had won the match. East blamed West who blamed the cruel trump break.

Both were right. The distribution was unkind, yet West should have made the slam.

He needed one more trick somewhere and this was the time to think of a squeeze. Suppose that the defender with four or more hearts also had the ◇ K. Wouldn't he squirm as he followed to all those spades? Undoubtedly, but there was just one snag. Dummy would be squeezed before South. To put matters right, West should play off dummy's ◇ A, an unblocking play, known as the *Vienna Coup*. Now both dummy's low diamonds can be discarded and South is threatened by the ◇ Q in declarer's hand and the four hearts on the table.

The next hand is taken from an 'O' level examination—not for pupils, but for bridge teachers. Many men and women teach bridge, but not all, by any means, are qualified. To make sure that those who set out to instruct others are proficient themselves, the English Bridge Union set up in 1970 the Teachers' Training Scheme. Local and educational authorities, looking for teachers, have been making good use of it.

Candidates in an examination were asked to comment on the bidding below.

Dealer South: Both Vul.

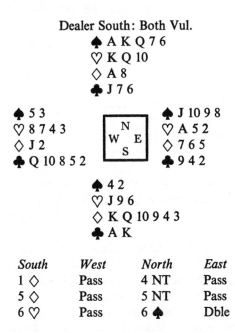

♠ A K Q 7 6
♥ K Q 10
♦ A 8
♣ J 7 6

♠ 5 3
♥ 8 7 4 3
♦ J 2
♣ Q 10 8 5 2

♠ J 10 9 8
♥ A 5 2
♦ 7 6 5
♣ 9 4 2

♠ 4 2
♥ J 9 6
♦ K Q 10 9 4 3
♣ A K

South	West	North	East
1 ♦	Pass	4 NT	Pass
5 ♦	Pass	5 NT	Pass
6 ♥	Pass	6 ♠	Dble

Would the reader like to pass judgment?

First, let's have North in the dock. His dizzy leap to 4 NT, enquiring for aces before a suit had been agreed, is the classical way not to use Blackwood. Guilty? Very.

Next comes East—if he hasn't jumped his bail. The only slam he could be reasonably sure to defeat was in spades, so his double stood to gain 100 and to lose 1,440 by driving opponents into an unbeatable 6 NT. Guilty again? Certainly, but this time there will be a plea of diminished responsibility.

Tony Lederer, leading light of the Teachers' Training Scheme, tells me that bridge is viewed in the most favourable light by prison authorities, who look upon it as excellent remedial therapy.

Some of the inmates take courses and become qualified teachers, even if they cannot practise—as yet.

Those who take a teachers' course have to pass a written examination, then an oral test which involves lecturing for twenty minutes.

Tony and Rhoda Lederer often visit the prisons themselves. One of their most promising pupils, now a qualified teacher, is serving a life sentence in the Grendon Psychiatric Prison at Aylesbury. When he qualified, he had another eight years to go. This was a problem he solved in a matter of seconds.

```
♠ 7 4                        ♠ A Q 6 2
♡ A K Q J 10 6    N          ♡ 5 4
◇ A 10 2       W     E       ◇ 9 7 6
♣ 4 3             S          ♣ K Q 6 3
```

North leads the ◇ K. How should declarer play?

Declarer's natural reflex is to allow West to hold the ◇ K in the hope of cutting enemy communications. Usually that's right. Here it could be fatal, if North switches to a spade.

If the ♣ A is right, declarer won't need the spade finesse, but he must retain the ♠ A in dummy as a vital entry to the clubs.

The venue for the next hand was the United States Federal Penitentiary in Kansas and the occasion was the annual pairs event to which the inmates—who have regular weekly duplicates among themselves—are allowed to invite guests from outside.

Several declarers brought home 4 ♠ on South's cards, after East had opened as dealer with 3 ♣.

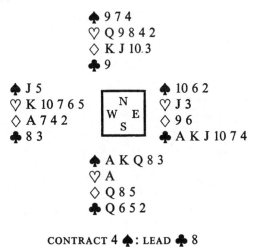

♠ 9 7 4
♡ Q 9 8 4 2
◇ K J 10 3
♣ 9

♠ J 5
♡ K 10 7 6 5
◇ A 7 4 2
♣ 8 3

♠ 10 6 2
♡ J 3
◇ 9 6
♣ A K J 10 7 4

♠ A K Q 8 3
♡ A
◇ Q 8 5
♣ Q 6 5 2

CONTRACT 4 ♠ : LEAD ♣ 8

East wins and returns the ♡ J to the ♡ A. Two rounds of trumps follow. Without seeing all four hands, how should declarer play?

From the bidding, it is clear that East cannot have the ◇ A as well as good, long clubs. The play marks West with the ♡ K. So declarer ruffs a club—an unavoidable risk—ruffs a heart and picks up the last trump. He then leads a diamond and West is helpless.

Most of the prisoners—or their guests—held up the ◇ A twice and returned the ♡ K. This was allowed to hold and with red cards only left, West had to put dummy in for the fulfilling trick.

The Kansas hand, reported in New York's *Bridge World*, is taken from real life. The next one, in the same magazine, conjures up an imaginary match in Alcatraz and shows how unscrupulous players can benefit by deriving improper information without breaking the law.

Dealer East: Love All

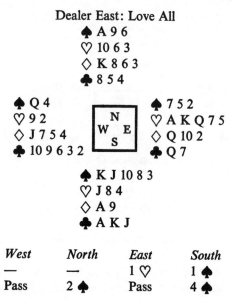

♠ A 9 6
♡ 10 6 3
◇ K 8 6 3
♣ 8 5 4

♠ Q 4
♡ 9 2
◇ J 7 5 4
♣ 10 9 6 3 2

♠ 7 5 2
♡ A K Q 7 5
◇ Q 10 2
♣ Q 7

♠ K J 10 8 3
♡ J 8 4
◇ A 9
♣ A K J

West	North	East	South
—	—	1 ♡	1 ♠
Pass	2 ♠	Pass	4 ♠

West leads the ♡ 9 to East's ♡ K. The ♡ A and ♡ Q follow.

The contract hinges on finding the ♠ Q, but an inmate of Alcatraz improves the odds. He ruffs the third round of hearts with the ♠ J and waits. As West over-ruffs, partner asks: 'No hearts?'

'Hearts? Oh yes, I have one,' admits South. The ♠ J and ♠ Q are thereupon withdrawn.

Before the revoke has been established—that is before the offending side plays to the next trick—there is no penalty. But will declarer now fail to find the ♠ Q? With the law as it is, he can profit handsomely from his 'lapse'.

The last four hands have no seasonal significance, but as our cavalcade crosses the Channel it's still spring.

This was a hand played at The Hague in the Common Market Championship of 1973, the first in which Britain took part.

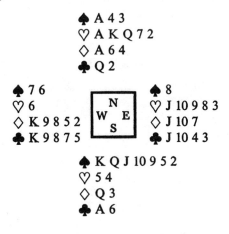

♠ A 4 3
♡ A K Q 7 2
◇ A 6 4
♣ Q 2

♠ 7 6
♡ 6
◇ K 9 8 5 2
♣ K 9 8 7 5

♠ 8
♡ J 10 9 8 3
◇ J 10 7
♣ J 10 4 3

♠ K Q J 10 9 5 2
♡ 5 4
◇ Q 3
♣ A 6

CONTRACT 7 ♠ : LEAD ♡ 6

The same hands were played at all the tables and several Souths reached 7 ♠.

Not seeing the other hands, declarer hopes, naturally, to set up a long heart for his thirteenth trick. After drawing trumps in two rounds, he tests the hearts and learns the bad news. No hope there. Can he still bring home the grand slam?

Several stars, including Blue Team champions Garozzo and Belladonna, made the contract; but the biggest round of applause was for Holland's Bob Slavenburg, who played the hand at top speed.

No technician should falter in this situation and world champion Bob Slavenburg barely paused for breath.

After taking the top hearts and throwing the ♣ 6 from his hand, he laid down the ♣ A and played out his trumps. When the last one appeared, at the eleventh trick, he remained with the ◇ Q 3 facing dummy's ◇ A 6, ♣ Q, and West had to play first—to bare his ◇ K or let go the ♣ K.

April is the time for the Riviera, so we move to the Open Pairs at Cannes.

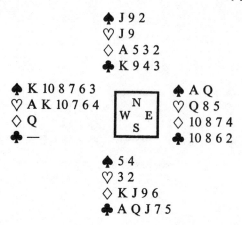

♠ J 9 2
♡ J 9
◇ A 5 3 2
♣ K 9 4 3

♠ K 10 8 7 6 3   ♠ A Q
♡ A K 10 7 6 4   ♡ Q 8 5
◇ Q   ◇ 10 8 7 4
♣ —   ♣ 10 8 6 2

♠ 5 4
♡ 3 2
◇ K J 9 6
♣ A Q J 7 5

Only one East-West pair, apparently, reached the cast-iron slam. Yet natural methods—shunned by many experts these days —should get there easily.

West	East
1 ♠	1 NT
4 ♡	5 ♡
6 ♡	—

East has eight points only—at first. But when West shows his freak two-suiter, this soars to twelve or more, for every point works.

French champions, José Le Dentu and Leon Tintner, sat North-South against two benign old ladies. West opened 1 ♠ and after two passes Le Dentu made what he calls: 'The best balancing bid of my career'. He reopened with 2 ♣. In a matter of seconds the old ladies were on the way to a slam.

'I passed 1 ♠,' explained East, 'because we play the Big Club, so with sixteen points, partner would have opened 1 ♣. And with fewer than twenty-four we couldn't have game, could we?'

A slam? Well, that was different. The experts smiled wanly.

The underdog enjoys much sympathy, if little else. But who will shed a tear for the strong ensnared by the innocence of the weak?

In May, the scene shifts a few miles down the coast to Juan-les-

Pins. Here is a top for the British international, Jonathan Cansino, playing with world champion, Joan Durran.

Dealer South: Love All

♠ A Q 5
♡ A 6 4 2
◇ 7
♣ K Q 10 9 4

♠ J 9 8 7 6
♡ K Q 10 9
◇ K Q 6
♣ 6

♠ 10
♡ 8 7 5 3
◇ J 10 9 5 2
♣ 5 3 2

♠ K 4 3 2
♡ J
◇ A 8 4 3
♣ A J 8 7

South	West	North	East
Cansino		J. Durran	
1 ♣	1 ♠	2 ♠	Pass
2 NT	Pass	4 ♣	Pass
4 ◇	Pass	4 ♡	Pass
4 ♠	Pass	5 ◇	Pass
5 ♡	Pass	5 ♠	Pass
5 NT	Pass	7 ♣	

All first- and second-round controls having been pin-pointed, Cansino bid 5 NT, the conventional grand slam force 'Josephine', asking partner to bid seven of the agreed suit if she had two of the three top honours. Joan Durran duly called the grand slam to which her fine bidding had paved the way.

West led the ♡ K. There are only ten top tricks, but Cansino made three more by means of a dummy reversal. Going up with the ♡ A, he ruffed a heart, crossed to dummy with a trump and ruffed another heart. Returning to the table with a spade, he ruffed dummy's fourth heart with his last trump and laid down the ◇ A. The stage was set to ruff a diamond and draw trumps from dummy.

To Deauville in July for the *Tournoi des Champions*, one of the most exclusive pairs events in the world, the *Sunday Times* being the other.

This was the problem which confronted North on the most sensational hand in the tournament of 1972.

♠ K Q 10 7 6 4
♡ —
◇ A Q 7 6
♣ 9 6 3

What should he lead against 7 ♡ after this sequence?

South	West	North	East
1 ♠	3 ♡	4 ♡	5 ♡
Pass	Pass	6 ♠	7 ♡
Dble			

Assuming that opponents were sacrificing, North was concerned not so much with defeating the contract as with extracting the maximum penalty. So he led the ♠ K. This was the full deal:

♠ K Q 10 7 6 4
♡ —
◇ A Q 7 6
♣ 9 6 3

♠ 9
♡ Q 8 7 6 4 3 2
◇ 9
♣ A 8 5 3

♠ —
♡ A K 10 5
◇ J 5 4 2
♣ K Q J 7 4

♠ A J 8 5 3 2
♡ J 9
◇ K 10 8 2
♣ 10

Harold Ogust, the American declarer, ruffed in dummy, drew trumps, and discarding his ◇ 9 on dummy's fifth club, claimed 1,770.

At the next table, the French international, Leclery, under-bid deceptively on North's hand. The auction started the same way, but anticipating vigorous competition, Leclery contented himself with a mere 4 ♠ over West's 3 ♡. Thereafter opponents weren't sure which side was sacrificing and South ended up playing in 6 ♠ doubled, scoring 1,660—a difference of 3,430 between the two tables.

Winners of the tournament that year, were Canada's Murray and Kehela. Here they are defending against France's Paul Chemla, who was South.

Dealer North: E/W Vul.

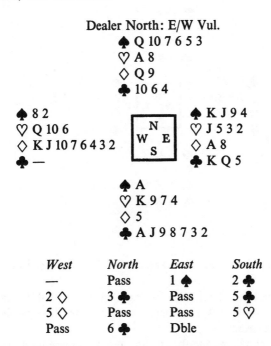

```
                    ♠ Q 10 7 6 5 3
                    ♡ A 8
                    ◇ Q 9
                    ♣ 10 6 4
  ♠ 8 2                                ♠ K J 9 4
  ♡ Q 10 6           N                 ♡ J 5 3 2
  ◇ K J 10 7 6 4 3 2  W     E          ◇ A 8
  ♣ —                   S              ♣ K Q 5
                    ♠ A
                    ♡ K 9 7 4
                    ◇ 5
                    ♣ A J 9 8 7 3 2
```

West	North	East	South
—	Pass	1 ♠	2 ♣
2 ◇	3 ♣	Pass	5 ♣
5 ◇	Pass	Pass	5 ♡
Pass	6 ♣	Dble	

West leads the ♠ 8. Can the contract be made?

Chemla began by covering the ♠ 8 with dummy's ♠ 10. Not knowing whether declarer's ♠ A was bare or whether he had the ♠ 2 behind it, Kehela, East, covered. Crossing to the ♡ A, Chemla led the ♠ Q, covered and ruffed.

The ♡ K and a heart ruff followed, then the ♠ 7, again covered and ruffed. Declarer now ruffed his last heart and discarded, the ◇ 5 on dummy's ♠ 5. All that remained was to run the ♣ 10, when Kehela refused to cover.

August is a quiet month, but history was made in 1971 when the Richmond Charity Congress, in aid of Action for the Crippled Child, moved to the West End and, sponsored by the *Evening Standard*, broke the London attendance record at the first attempt.

Founder of the Congress was David Rex-Taylor. His partner here was British international, Marjorie Whitaker, sitting South.

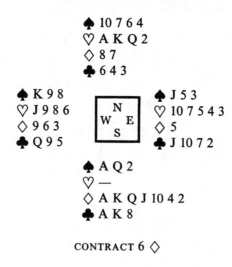

CONTRACT 6 ◇

West leads a low club. How should South make certain of the contract?

If South had the ◇ 9 instead of the ◇ 4 or ◇ 2, all would be plain sailing. As things are, there's no access to three perfectly good tricks in hearts.

Marjorie Whitaker soon found the solution. Going up with the ♣ A, she played a *low* trump, allowing West to take a wholly unexpected trick with the ◇ 9. Thereafter, however, the ◇ 8 provided an entry to the ♡ A K Q and all was well.

Most North-South pairs at the first *Evening Standard* Bridge Congress reached 4 ♠ on:

Dealer North: Love All

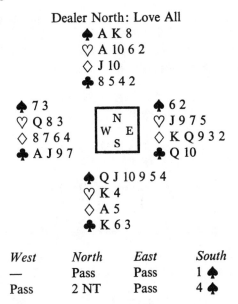

♠ A K 8
♡ A 10 6 2
◇ J 10
♣ 8 5 4 2

♠ 7 3   ♠ 6 2
♡ Q 8 3   ♡ J 9 7 5
◇ 8 7 6 4   ◇ K Q 9 3 2
♣ A J 9 7   ♣ Q 10

♠ Q J 10 9 5 4
♡ K 4
◇ A 5
♣ K 6 3

West	North	East	South
—	Pass	Pass	1 ♠
Pass	2 NT	Pass	4 ♠

That was the usual sequence. And at every table but one declarer lost a diamond and three clubs. The exception was world champion, Joan Durran, who made the contract.

She allowed East to hold the first diamond. Coming in with the ◇ A at trick two, she played two rounds of hearts and ruffed a heart. After a spade to the ♠ A, she ruffed dummy's last heart, drew the remaining trumps with the ♠ K and led a club. East played the ♣ 10 and Joan ducked. Now the defence was helpless. If West overtakes the ♣ Q, which follows, declarer scores the ♣ K. If East remains on play, whichever red card he leads presents declarer with a ruff and discard.

Why did Joan Durran play West rather than East for the ♣ A? Because East had shown up already with the ◇ K Q and the ♡ J. He was less likely to have the missing ace.

Yes, if East goes up at once with the ♣ Q, the contract is defeated. It's an easy defence, double-dummy, not quite so easy at the table.

A hand with a most unexpected result came up the same year, in an event entitled 'Play with an International Pair'. In this, all the East-Wests have an anchor pair of internationals as their North-South team-mates. All the other North-Souths have two internationals as their East-West pair. It is essentially a pairs event with teams-of-four scoring.

Dealer West: N/S Vul.

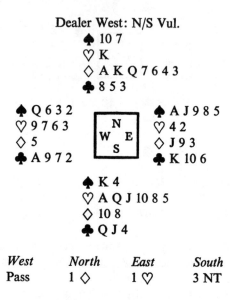

♠ 10 7
♡ K
◇ A K Q 7 6 4 3
♣ 8 5 3

♠ Q 6 3 2
♡ 9 7 6 3
◇ 5
♣ A 9 7 2

♠ A J 9 8 5
♡ 4 2
◇ J 9 3
♣ K 10 6

♠ K 4
♡ A Q J 10 8 5
◇ 10 8
♣ Q J 4

West	North	East	South
Pass	1 ◇	1 ♡	3 NT

Without East's psychic overcall in hearts, West would have led a black suit and declarer would have doubtless made ten tricks. On a heart lead, strange things happened. Declarer won with dummy's lone king and anxiously laid down the ◇ A. When all followed, he beamed and claimed thirteen tricks, announcing that he would take seven diamonds and six hearts.

'Play them,' demanded East.

Long before he reached the last diamond which he had to play, South realized what he had done. Reduced to five cards he had to unguard one of three suits. He couldn't bear the ignominy of losing a heart, so he let go a club. One down.

A very different way of teaming up with the experts is the *Play with the Masters* tournament, held annually by the Jewish National Fund's Charity Trust. Most of London's leading players, Jews and Gentiles alike, gather for the occasion.

The competitors buy tickets to play with the masters. A draw for partners is followed by a spirited auction in which a fancied pair fetches £100 or more. Prizes are awarded for the highest scores. This was one of my earliest experiences in this event.

Dealer West: Love All

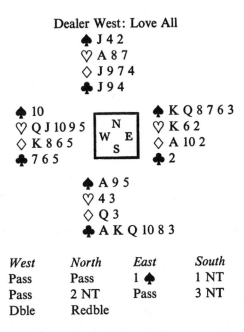

West	North	East	South
Pass	Pass	1 ♠	1 NT
Pass	2 NT	Pass	3 NT
Dble	Redble		

I was South, West, a nervous young man, who had drawn a redoubtable lady champion, led the ♠ 10. I covered in dummy and allowed East's ♠ Q to hold. Thereafter, the marked spade finesse ensured the contract.

'Why did you double?' enquired the R.L.C. belligerently. 'And what made you pick the only card in your hand to give them the contract?'

'I led *your* suit,' replied West reverently. 'I knew that if you bid it, I should lead it—and double.'

'And I knew', retorted my partner, 'that if you played the hand, I should redouble.'

How wrong they both were.

Overseas again for the Don Pepe tournament in Marbella. At

both tables the contract is 6 NT. Blue Team veteran, Camillo Pabis-Ticci is declarer in one room. Spanish international, Señora Paternina is South in the other.

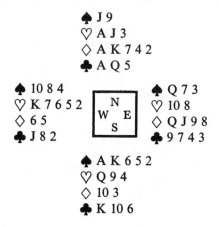

```
                    ♠ J 9
                    ♡ A J 3
                    ♢ A K 7 4 2
                    ♣ A Q 5
   ♠ 10 8 4                         ♠ Q 7 3
   ♡ K 7 6 5 2      N               ♡ 10 8
   ♢ 6 5         W     E            ♢ Q J 9 8
   ♣ J 8 2          S               ♣ 9 7 4 3
                    ♠ A K 6 5 2
                    ♡ Q 9 4
                    ♢ 10 3
                    ♣ K 10 6
```

West led the ♢ 6. Pabis-Ticci went up with the ♢ A, crossed to his hand with a club and led a spade to dummy's ♠ J, and East's ♠ Q. Capturing the diamond return, he cashed his winners carefully observing the discards, for somehow he would have to make three hearts. On the long spades West shed two hearts, East a diamond and a club. Now the ♡ Q, towards dummy, allowed Pabis-Ticci to catch West's ♡ K and scoop East's ♡ 10. Inspired play.

In the other room the first trick was the same, but then Señora Paternina, playing quickly and with assurance, led the ♠ J. Not suspecting a confidence trick, East played low and it was all over in a flash. Had South the ♠ 10, as seemed certain, East couldn't gain by covering and there was a chance that declarer would play for the drop. Brazen, but effective.

'Much depends,' observes *Le Bridgeur*, 'on whether declarer is a man or a woman.'

In 1974, despite the presence of the *squadra azzurra*, the team event at Marbella was won by Omar Sharif's Circus, representing France.

Omar, partnered by Paul Chemla, was sitting South here, opposing Italy's Camillo Pabis-Ticci and Walter Avarelli.

Dealer South: Both Vul.

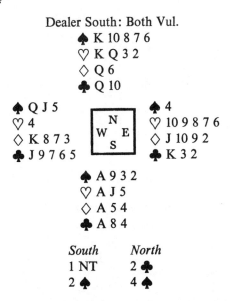

♠ K 10 8 7 6
♡ K Q 3 2
◇ Q 6
♣ Q 10

♠ Q J 5　　　　　　　♠ 4
♡ 4　　　　　　　　　♡ 10 9 8 7 6
◇ K 8 7 3　　　　　　◇ J 10 9 2
♣ J 9 7 6 5　　　　　♣ K 3 2

♠ A 9 3 2
♡ A J 5
◇ A 5 4
♣ A 8 4

South	North
1 NT	2 ♣
2 ♠	4 ♠

How many tricks could Omar expect to make after the lead of the ♣ 6?

This is what happened.

Omar played the ♣ 10 from dummy and took the ♣ K with his ♣ A. After two rounds of trumps had revealed the 3–1 break, he cashed the ♣ Q, crossed to the ♡ A and ruffed his third club. Next he played out the hearts.

West wouldn't oblige by ruffing, but it didn't help him, for having eliminated the hearts and clubs, Omar threw him in with a trump, forcing him to lead a diamond away from his ◇ K or else concede a ruff and discard.

Inexorably Omar Sharif made twelve tricks.

In the other room Belladonna and Vivaldi bid a highly ambitious 6 ♠ and went two down.

Justice was done.

It's nearer from Marbella to Hong Kong by jet today than it was from London to Paris by coach yesterday, so here we are at the Far Eastern Championships, contested by thirteen nations.

Playing as guests of honour, Jeremy Flint and Irving Rose won the Pairs. This was one of their tops.

Dealer West: Love All

♠ 8 2
♡ 10 8 5 3
♢ 3 2
♣ Q J 6 4 2

```
        N
   W        E
        S
```

♠ K 7
♡ A 6
♢ A K J 10 9
♣ A 10 8 3

West	North	East	South
1 ♠	Pass	1 NT	Dble
2 ♠	Pass	Pass	3 ♢
Pass	Pass	Dble	

West led the ♣ 7 to dummy's ♣ Q, East's ♣ K and Rose's ♣ A. Taking advantage of the lucky lead, how should declarer play?

Rose reasoned that East must have five diamonds for his double. If so, he couldn't draw trumps without losing the lead. Then a spade through his ♠ K would force him to ruff on the third round and thereafter dummy's fifth club would stay out of reach.

Rose found an elegant solution. At trick two he led the ♢ J!

♠ A Q 10 9 6 3   ♠ J 5 4
♡ K J 4 2   N   ♡ Q 9 7
♢ 4   W   E   ♢ Q 8 7 6 5
♣ 7 5   S   ♣ K 9

If East won, declarer couldn't be forced in spades for there would still be a trump in dummy. If he ducked, Rose would cross to the ♣ J, finesse, cash the ♢ A K and play clubs, scoring five trumps, three clubs—East would ruff the fourth one—and the ♡ A.

Christmas is upon us. Rixi Markus, the World Bridge Federation's 'First Lady' has a busy time. For three days, including Christmas Eve, while Santa Claus is packing his gifts, she presides over the Cutty Sark–*Guardian* Tournament. Then, on Boxing Day, she welcomes competitors to the *Harper's Queen* Winter Pairs.

True to the title of one of her books, Rixi *Bid*(s) *Boldly* (some say too boldly) *Play*(s) *Safely*—that no one disputes.

Here's an example.

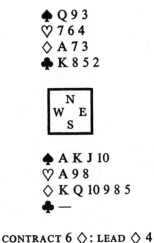

♠ Q 9 3
♡ 7 6 4
◇ A 7 3
♣ K 8 5 2

```
      N
  W       E
      S
```

♠ A K J 10
♡ A 9 8
◇ K Q 10 9 8 5
♣ —

CONTRACT 6 ◇ : LEAD ◇ 4

On dummy's ◇ 3, East plays the ◇ J. How should declarer play? Ready? Then let's follow Rixi.

At trick two, she led a low heart, the key play, for she couldn't afford a second round of trumps. Winning the trump return on which West showed out, with dummy's ◇ 7, Rixi led a club. With the ♣ A, East might be tempted. He wasn't, but one chance remained—that the defender with the third trump had four spades, which he did.

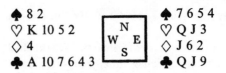

♠ 8 2
♡ K 10 5 2
♢ 4
♣ A 10 7 6 4 3

♠ 7 6 5 4
♡ Q J 3
♢ J 6 2
♣ Q J 9

Now Rixi Markus could discard a heart from dummy on her fourth spade and ruff a heart.

This was my first Christmas Eve contribution to the *Evening Standard*.

'What will Santa Claus bring us tomorrow? A welcome gift would be a grand slam at a critical moment in a key match. Our side is trailing, but we bring off a spectacular coup, make our slam and win the match. This is the stuff that dreams are made of, but it all happened in the finals of the Reisinger Trophy, one of America's big tournaments.

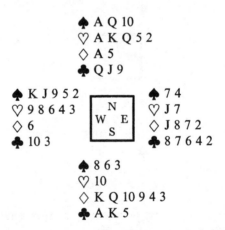

♠ A Q 10
♡ A K Q 5 2
♢ A 5
♣ Q J 9

♠ K J 9 5 2
♡ 9 8 6 4 3
♢ 6
♣ 10 3

♠ 7 4
♡ J 7
♢ J 8 7 2
♣ 8 7 6 4 2

♠ 8 6 3
♡ 10
♢ K Q 10 9 4 3
♣ A K 5

'The team that was in front finished in 7 NT and was defeated by the 4–1 diamond split. In the other room, South played in 7 ♢.

'West opened a heart. Since only a bad trump break could beat him, declarer thought of it from the start. He led a trump to his king, then another to dummy's ace. When West showed out, his foresight was rewarded. He ruffed a heart, played off the clubs, ending in dummy, and ruffed a second heart. He had reduced his trumps to East's length but he still needed two entries in dummy.

So he finessed the spade and led hearts, ready to over-ruff East's ◇ J. When East ruffed was immaterial.

'May the reader find such dream gifts in his stocking tomorrow.' This was another seasonal piece.

Santa Claus brings North-South an exciting Christmas present. Rising to the occasion, they quickly bid a grand slam in no trumps. How they got there we don't know. Maybe East-West sacrificed in 7 ♠ against 7 ◇. The point of the hand, however, is in the play.

West leads a spade. Before reading the text below, take South's hand and plan the play.

♠ —
♡ A
◇ A K Q
♣ A J 10 9 8 7 5 3 2

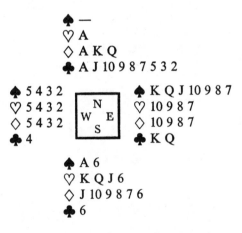

♠ 5 4 3 2
♡ 5 4 3 2
◇ 5 4 3 2
♣ 4

♠ K Q J 10 9 8 7
♡ 10 9 8 7
◇ 10 9 8 7
♣ K Q

♠ A 6
♡ K Q J 6
◇ J 10 9 8 7 6
♣ 6

CONTRACT 7 NT: LEAD ♠ 5

Normally, of course, we should be holding West's cards. But this is the Christmas season. Even so, we can only see twelve tricks—four hearts, six diamonds and the two black aces. Worse still, both the hearts and diamonds are blocked in dummy. What can we do about it and where do we find the thirteenth trick?

The solution lies in discarding the ♡ A at trick one, taken by the ♠ A. This costs a trick, but now the ◇ A K Q can be thrown on the ♡ K Q J and the diamonds are unblocked. South reels them off, leaving himself with ♠ 6 ♡ 6 ♣ 6. What can poor East throw on the last diamond? Whether it's his last heart or his last spade, South will play the six of the suit, forcing East to surrender.

The reindeer sweeping past us, with red-nosed Rudolf in the lead, bring the cavalcade to an end. Before the chimes of Big Ben usher in the New Year, bridge writers ponder and decide which was the best hand during the previous twelve months. Entries from the world over are submitted to the International Bridge Press Association which makes an award at its annual meeting.

I close this chapter with four of the entries which I picked for my own column.

The first is from a tournament in Los Angeles, reported in *Popular Bridge*.

♠ A 7
♡ A 6
♢ A 5 4
♣ A K 9 7 6 4

♠ Q 4
♡ K Q J 10 8 7 5 4
♢ 9 7 3
♣ —

CONTRACT 7 ♡: LEAD ♢ K

Winning with the ♢ A, declarer counted his tricks. He could see twelve on top and needed, therefore, to develop one more in clubs. If the clubs broke 4–3, there would be no trouble, and if they were 6–1, there would be no hope. So South concentrated on the third possibility, a 5–2 break. To find out the position, he led at once the ♣ A K and ruffed a third club. West showed out and now declarer needed three entries in dummy to ruff two more clubs and get back to enjoy the last one. Unfortunately, only two entries were available, the ♠ A and the ♡ A. To create a third one, South led the ♡ 4 and finessed. The ♡ 6 held and all was well.

Transpose the ♡ 6 and ♡ 5 and now West can foil declarer by going up with the ♡ 9.

In 1972, the late Alan Sobel, for many years America's premier tournament director, gave his award to this elegant dummy play, featured by Alan Truscott in the *New York Times*.

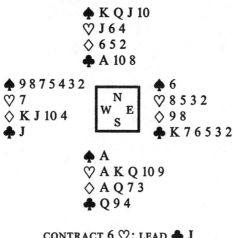

                    ♠ K Q J 10
                    ♡ J 6 4
                    ◊ 6 5 2
                    ♣ A 10 8

♠ 9 8 7 5 4 3 2   ♠ 6
♡ 7   ♡ 8 5 3 2
◊ K J 10 4   ◊ 9 8
♣ J   ♣ K 7 6 5 3 2

                    ♠ A
                    ♡ A K Q 10 9
                    ◊ A Q 7 3
                    ♣ Q 9 4

CONTRACT 6 ♡: LEAD ♣ J

Truscott invites the reader to look at all four hands and treat the deal as a double-dummy problem.

This is usually the solver's first attempt: he goes up with the ♣ A—to duck would obviously be fatal—cashes the ♠ A and continues with three rounds of trumps, ending in dummy. Next comes the ♣ 8, and on East's ♣ K, he throws his ♣ Q, creating a club entry in dummy.

It won't work. East wins the day by returning another club, while he still has a trump. Alternatively, he can hold up his ♣ K.

No, the hand can only be made at trick one. South must jettison his ♣ Q at once! Now he can take four rounds of trumps, before leading a club. No matter what East does, he cannot keep South out of dummy.

The following year, this was the choice of *Le Figaro*'s José Le Dentu.

Dealer East: N/S Vul.

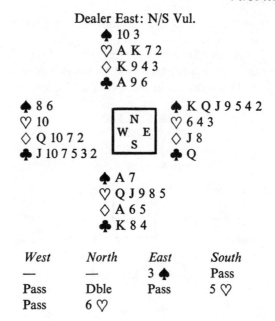

West	*North*	*East*	*South*
—	—	3 ♠	Pass
Pass	Dble	Pass	5 ♡
Pass	6 ♡		

South only just managed to pass over East's pre-emptive 3 ♠ and naturally envisaged a slam when North found values to re-open with a take-out double. The jump to 5 ♡ focused attention on the quality of the prospective trumps, and holding ♡ A K, North gladly accepted the invitation. West led the ♠ 8.

South appears to have three losers, but things aren't always what they seem. When East follows three times in hearts, prospects quickly improve. Declarer cashes the ♣ K, the ♢ A and ♢ K, and puts East on play with a spade. He cannot help returning another spade, which South ruffs in dummy, discarding from hand his third diamond. Getting back with a diamond ruff, it only remains for him to lead his last trump.

Three cards remain: West has the ♢ Q and ♣ J 10. Poised over him in dummy are the ♢ 3 and ♣ A 9—and it's West's turn to play.

This hand from Indonesia, submitted in 1974, stars seventeen-year-old Oscar Irawan.

Dealer North: Both Vul.

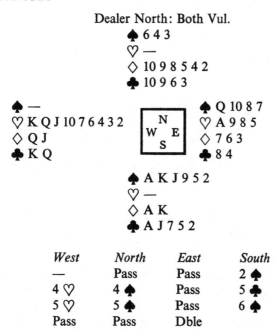

♠ 6 4 3
♡ —
♢ 10 9 8 5 4 2
♣ 10 9 6 3

♠ —
♡ K Q J 10 7 6 4 3 2
♢ Q J
♣ K Q

♠ Q 10 8 7
♡ A 9 8 5
♢ 7 6 3
♣ 8 4

♠ A K J 9 5 2
♡ —
♢ A K
♣ A J 7 5 2

West	North	East	South
—	Pass	Pass	2 ♠
4 ♡	4 ♠	Pass	5 ♣
5 ♡	5 ♠	Pass	6 ♠
Pass	Pass	Dble	

West led the ♡ K and declarer pondered deeply. East's double proclaimed four spades and there was a certain club loser. Was there any hope?

Irawan decided that the contract could be made, though only if the lie of the cards was as above, and he proceeded to play accordingly.

He ruffed the ♡ K with dummy's ♠ 6 and under-ruffed with his ♠ 5. Next he took the deep finesse in trumps, cashed the ♢ A K and continued with the ♣ A and ♣ 2.

West had to exit with a heart and once again declarer ruffed in dummy and under-ruffed with the ♠ 2 in his hand. It only remained to lead diamonds. In the three-card ending, with the lead in dummy, South would sit with ♠ A K J over East's ♠ Q 10 8.

As we tear off the last page of the calendar, the first interval comes to a close and we return to the world stage where the curtain is about to rise for Act II.

ACT II

The Blue Phoenix rises from the ashes
C. C. Wei defies the laws of gravity

We left Ira Corn's Aces triumphant at Taipeh. Their reign wasn't destined to last much longer.

Rising from the ashes, the Blue Phoenix soared higher than ever before, driving the American eagles from their eyries.

The sudden reincarnation of the invincible *squadra azzurra* coincided with another fateful event in modern history—the birth of Precision, conceived by the Chinese tanker owner, Charles Wei.

Everything about Wei's brainchild defies the laws of gravity.

All other bidding systems have been forged in the crucible of top-class bridge by players of renown. Charles Wei has no pretensions as a player.

Culbertson, Goren, lesser lights in Europe, all made money out of their systems. To learn the secrets of success the public had to buy their books, read their ghosted articles, attend their schools.

Charles Wei has no need of money and no wish to make a penny out of bridge. On the contrary, he pays money to converts and has often rewarded with a bonus the winners of tournaments—provided that they played Precision.

'The Prostitution Club' sneered the cynics, but it wasn't long before the mighty Blue Club, and the Roman, were overhauled in public esteem by a system of which no one had ever heard until an obscure team from Taiwan beat the pride of America into third place in the World Championship of 1969 in Brazil.

Technically, the Chinese were outclassed, but the simple virtues of Precision allowed them to score many points against their more sophisticated opponents.

Here's an example from their first spectacular success in Rio, featuring what the Americans call 'the gambling 3 NT'. Tai and Huang sat East and West.

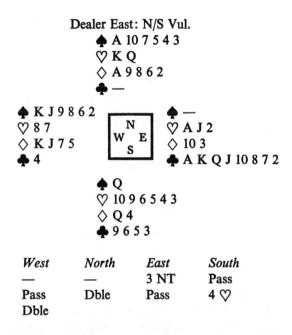

Dealer East: N/S Vul.

♠ A 10 7 5 4 3
♡ K Q
◇ A 9 8 6 2
♣ —

♠ K J 9 8 6 2   ♠ —
♡ 8 7   ♡ A J 2
◇ K J 7 5   ◇ 10 3
♣ 4   ♣ A K Q J 10 8 7 2

♠ Q
♡ 10 9 6 5 4 3
◇ Q 4
♣ 9 6 5 3

West	North	East	South
—	—	3 NT	Pass
Pass	Dble	Pass	4 ♡
Dble			

Had Walter Avarelli, North, passed 3 NT, he might well have missed a vulnerable game. So he doubled. It was a guess either way and this one cost 1,100.

One turns page after page of the records without finding another example of a 1,100 penalty by the Blue Team. The 'gambling 3 NT' forced them to gamble, and gamblers cannot always win.

A 3 NT opening, based on a long solid minor, has been part of Acol, the British system, for many years, but usually there are no outside values. Here the ♡ A would be considered *de trop*.

Like all artificial systems, Precision leads, at times, to misunderstandings. Then it needs gifted improvization to avoid disaster, as on this deal from the World Championship in 1970, when the Formosans were again in the finals.

Dealer West: Love All

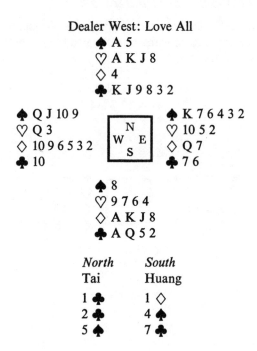

♠ A 5
♡ A K J 8
◇ 4
♣ K J 9 8 3 2

♠ Q J 10 9
♡ Q 3
◇ 10 9 6 5 3 2
♣ 10

♠ K 7 6 4 3 2
♡ 10 5 2
◇ Q 7
♣ 7 6

♠ 8
♡ 9 7 6 4
◇ A K J 8
♣ A Q 5 2

North	South
Tai	Huang
1 ♣	1 ◇
2 ♣	4 ♠
5 ♠	7 ♣

Tai's 1 ♣ promises sixteen points or more. Huang's 1 ◇ ostensibly denies eight points, but followed by the jump to 4 ♠ it is a specialized and artificial sequence, showing a strong three-suiter with a singleton in the suit bid, in this case, spades.

Alas, North misunderstood or forgot the convention. Hence his support for the non-existent spades. Patrick Huang's leap to 7 ♣, suggested an official commentator, was intended to prevent Tai from reverting to spades. As the cards lie, the grand slam is unbeatable, but what a curious way to reach it!

Without the benefit of a misunderstanding, the Americans in the other room stopped in 6 ♣.

The success of the Chinese was sensational and overnight Precision became the 'In-thing'.

Books on Precision flooded the market. Leading players took up the system, won tournaments and claimed the bonuses. And then came the coup of coups—the conversion to Precision of the Blue Team itself!

Katherine Wei, charismatic, electric, indefatigable, is quoted as saying: 'The wives of other rich men want jewels and furs. I want the Blue Team', and of course Kathy had her way.

The first of the Blues to be converted was Benito Garozzo. This was one of his earliest ventures in Precision. He is South in the diagram.

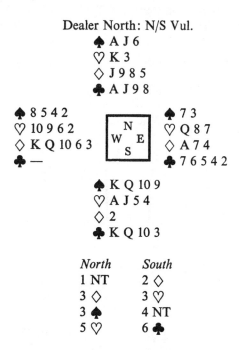

Dealer North: N/S Vul.

                ♠ A J 6
                ♡ K 3
                ◇ J 9 8 5
                ♣ A J 9 8

  ♠ 8 5 4 2   ♠ 7 3
  ♡ 10 9 6 2   N   ♡ Q 8 7
  ◇ K Q 10 6 3   W   E   ◇ A 7 4
  ♣ —   S   ♣ 7 6 5 4 2

                ♠ K Q 10 9
                ♡ A J 5 4
                ◇ 2
                ♣ K Q 10 3

North	South
1 NT	2 ◇
3 ◇	3 ♡
3 ♠	4 NT
5 ♡	6 ♣

It's odd to reach a slam in a suit first bid at the six level, but it's all part of the system. South's 2 ◇ is a variation on the Stayman theme, asking for a major and also proclaiming strength. North's 3 ◇ denies a major, but shows two minors. Having found the club fit, Garozzo exchanged cue-bids and sailed slamwards.

West opened the ◇ K which East overtook to lead a trump, revealing the 5–0 break. Garozzo was equal to it. Winning in dummy, he ruffed a diamond and went over with the ♡ K to ruff a second diamond. Next he cashed the ♠ K, the ♠ A and faced the critical decision—to take a third spade or the heart finesse.

Garozzo finessed—the better chance—discarded dummy's ♠ J and cross-ruffed the rest.

To spread the gospel, Kathy Wei embarked on a world tour, captaining a team which included Benito Garozzo and Giorgio Belladonna, Alan Truscott, Dorothy Hayden and Dimmie Fleming. They went, they were seen and they conquered, winning eleven of their twelve matches.

The biggest audiences were in South Africa where crowds of 500 watched nightly on Bridgerama.

Garozzo is South, once more.

Dealer North: Love All

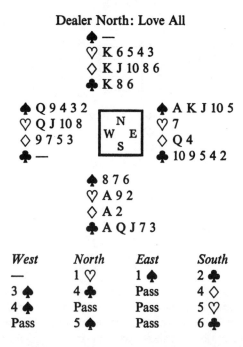

♠ —
♡ K 6 5 4 3
◇ K J 10 8 6
♣ K 8 6

♠ Q 9 4 3 2   ♠ A K J 10 5
♡ Q J 10 8   ♡ 7
◇ 9 7 5 3   ◇ Q 4
♣ —   ♣ 10 9 5 4 2

♠ 8 7 6
♡ A 9 2
◇ A 2
♣ A Q J 7 3

West	North	East	South
—	1 ♡	1 ♠	2 ♣
3 ♠	4 ♣	Pass	4 ◇
4 ♠	Pass	Pass	5 ♡
Pass	5 ♠	Pass	6 ♣

With bad breaks in hearts and clubs, the odds appear to be weighted against declarer, but when Benito Garozzo is in charge, things aren't always what they seem.

West opened a spade, ruffed in dummy. Anxious not to lose control, at trick two, Garozzo made the far-sighted play of the ◇ J. When East, somewhat perplexed, failed to cover, fortune changed sides. Returning to dummy with the ♣ K, after cashing the ◇ A, Benito went on leading diamonds. East eventually made a trump, but it was the only trick for his side.

Nowhere was the standard of play higher than in Thailand, where the Precision team trailed all the way, just managing to snatch victory on the last board. It would have stood no chance but for this hand on which Dorothy Hayden was North and Alan Truscott sat South.

Dealer South: E/W Vul.

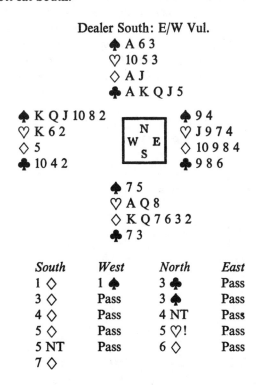

```
                    ♠ A 6 3
                    ♡ 10 5 3
                    ◇ A J
                    ♣ A K Q J 5
  ♠ K Q J 10 8 2                      ♠ 9 4
  ♡ K 6 2            N                ♡ J 9 7 4
  ◇ 5            W       E            ◇ 10 9 8 4
  ♣ 10 4 2           S               ♣ 9 8 6
                    ♠ 7 5
                    ♡ A Q 8
                    ◇ K Q 7 6 3 2
                    ♣ 7 3
```

South	West	North	East
1 ◇	1 ♠	3 ♣	Pass
3 ◇	Pass	3 ♠	Pass
4 ◇	Pass	4 NT	Pass
5 ◇	Pass	5 ♡!	Pass
5 NT	Pass	6 ◇	Pass
7 ◇			

The key bid was Dorothy Hayden's 5 ♡. She wanted to be in 7 ◇, if Truscott had the ◇ K Q, but having already invoked Blackwood, 5 NT would have been an enquiry for kings, not Josephine, the grand slam force. So, as a substitute, she resorted to 5 ♡, followed by 6 ◇, a sequence which Alan Truscott had no difficulty in interpreting correctly.

A clash for the world title between the reborn Blues and the victorious Aces couldn't be long delayed, and as a spectacular rehearsal for the deadly battles to come, a Grand Challenge Match, with 45,000 dollars in prize money, was billed for December 1971 at Las Vegas.

The Blue Team was to be at full strength. Going over to Precision, the rest of the old guard—Pietro Forquet, Walter Avarelli, Mimo D'Alelio and Camillo Pabis-Ticci—joined Giorgio and Benito in a crash programme of matches against the strongest opposition in Europe. November saw them in London, crushing a British team which included four converts to Precision, Jeremy Flint and Jonathan Cansino, Irving Rose and Rob Sheehan.

Here Belladonna and Avarelli sat North-South against Flint-Cansino.

Dealer West: Love All

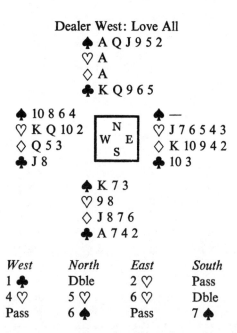

```
                    ♠ A Q J 9 5 2
                    ♡ A
                    ◇ A
                    ♣ K Q 9 6 5
  ♠ 10 8 6 4                        ♠ —
  ♡ K Q 10 2          N            ♡ J 7 6 5 4 3
  ◇ Q 5 3         W       E        ◇ K 10 9 4 2
  ♣ J 8               S            ♣ 10 3
                    ♠ K 7 3
                    ♡ 9 8
                    ◇ J 8 7 6
                    ♣ A 7 4 2
```

West	North	East	South
1 ♣	Dble	2 ♡	Pass
4 ♡	5 ♡	6 ♡	Dble
Pass	6 ♠	Pass	7 ♠

The basis of Precision is the 1 ♣ opening for hands with sixteen points or more. Doesn't Jeremy Flint, West, owe eight points, at least, for his opening? No. According to his variation, the 1 ♣

first or second in hand, non-vulnerable, may be weak or strong or average—mini, midi, maxi.

Cansino's 2 ♡ showed a six-card suit with 4–7 points. Having established a fit and abject weakness, the British pair tried hard to bounce the Italians out of a cold grand slam. It was not to be. Avarelli's double of 6 ♡ was constructive. Visualizing the ♣ A opposite, Belladonna bid 6 ♠, and if he could do that without the king of trumps, Avarelli, with it, could bid one more.

Ready for battle, with Katherine Wei as captain, the high-powered Precision team flew to Las Vegas.

Coinciding with what was advertised as the 'Match of the Century', the finals of America's first National Rubber Bridge Championship was held at the same hotel, the Hilton International. Ira Corn invited me to be the Director and it was this event which gave me my first hand from Las Vegas for the *Evening Standard*.

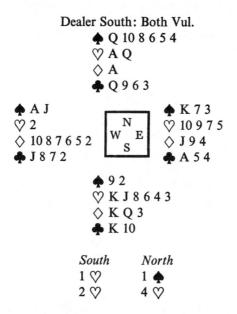

Dealer South: Both Vul.

```
            ♠ Q 10 8 6 5 4
            ♡ A Q
            ◇ A
            ♣ Q 9 6 3
♠ A J                      ♠ K 7 3
♡ 2           N            ♡ 10 9 7 5
◇ 10 8 7 6 5 2  W   E      ◇ J 9 4
♣ J 8 7 2        S         ♣ A 5 4
            ♠ 9 2
            ♡ K J 8 6 4 3
            ◇ K Q 3
            ♣ K 10
```

South	*North*
1 ♡	1 ♠
2 ♡	4 ♡

West led the ♣ 2 to East's ♣ A, won the spade switch with the ♠ A and returned the ♠ J.

South could see ten tricks, so long as he lost no trump. So he let the ♠ J ride. There was little hope for the defence, but East had one advantage. He knew, and declarer didn't, that the trumps were split 4–1. So he overtook the ♠ J with his ♠ K and returned his last spade.

Fearing an over-ruff, South trumped with the ♡ J, promoting East's ♡ 10 into a fully-fledged trick.

East-West went on to win the championship in which finalists of heats in thirty-one cities took part.

Meanwhile, the Challenge Match was under way. Both teams were much below form in the early stages, but while the Italians could afford their lapses, the Aces couldn't afford theirs, and before long the Blues drew away to win by a decisive margin.

Unlike the Italians, the Aces hadn't trained seriously for the match and they lacked the discipline and cohesion of their earlier performances. Neither was Las Vegas a happy venue for a team not all of whose members could resist the lure of the gaming tables.

Here are two notable Las Vegas slams.

Dealer North: Both Vul.

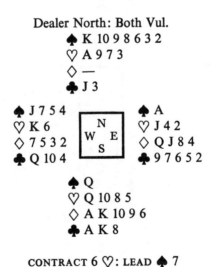

CONTRACT 6 ♡: LEAD ♠ 7

Paul Soloway, North, was a newcomer to the Aces and the hopeless slam was reached owing to a partnership misunderstanding.

Bob Hamman, declarer, won the club return at trick two with the ♣ A, and hoping to scoop a bare ♡ J, led the ♡ Q to the ♡ K and ♡ A. A second trump followed. Avarelli, East, went up with his ♡ J and Belladonna, West, . . . revoked.

With the help of two tricks, the penalty for a revoke, Hamman could have just made his contract, conceding two spades and a trump. Still unaware of his ♡ 6, however, Belladonna revoked again on the next trick, a third heart.

Confronted by the apparent 4-1 trump break, Hamman cut his losses, snatched what tricks he could, and went three down. As there is no penalty for a second revoke in the same suit, the first one went unpunished. One down.

Rarely has there been a better example of two wrongs making a right.

Bob Hamman had a happier part to play on the next hand.

Dealer West: E/W Vul.

```
                    ♠ K 6 5 2
                    ♡ J 7 5
                    ◇ Q 10 9
                    ♣ K 4 3
    ♠ 10 8 3                        ♠ Q J 9 4
    ♡ Q 3          ┌─────────┐      ♡ 9 4 2
    ◇ 6 4          │    N    │      ◇ 8 2
    ♣ A Q 9 8 7 2  │  W   E  │      ♣ J 10 6 5
                   │    S    │
                   └─────────┘
                    ♠ A 7
                    ♡ A K 10 8 6
                    ◇ A K J 7 5 3
                    ♣ —
```

West	North	East	South
Pass	Pass	Pass	1 ♣
Pass	1 ♡	Pass	2 ◇
Pass	3 ◇	Pass	3 ♡
Pass	3 ♠	Pass	4 ♣
Pass	4 ◇	Pass	7 ◇

The first round of bidding is artificial and follows the Blue Club pattern as played by the Aces.

The contract hinges on finding the ♡ Q, and with five cards missing, the odds favour a second-round finesse.

Hamman drew trumps, ending in dummy, and immediately led the ♡ J. His sixth sense was working overtime. Why didn't Avarelli cover?

Going up with the ♡ A, Hamman went back to dummy and led a second heart. He had made up his mind, and as soon as Avarelli played the ♡ 4, Hamman went up with the ♡ K, dropping West's ♡ Q.

Dropping doubleton honours isn't always due to card reading. Sometimes it's a matter of psychology, of sensing the vibrations round the table. Bob Hamman put out his antennae and found Walter Avarelli to be without the ♡ Q.

A few months after Las Vegas, the Blues demonstrated their superiority once again by a resounding victory in the fourth World Olympiad in Miami, an event rich in material for the connoisseur.

The clash, early in the qualifying stage of the Olympiad, between Italy's Blue Team and America's Aces was rightly regarded in Miami as a preview of the final.

There were big hands and big swings, all in Italy's favour, and a little luck, as well as a lot of skill, helped to swell the margin to 63–3. This board was worth 10 IMPs—International Match Points—to the *squadra azzurra.*

Dealer West: Love All

♠ A Q J 9
♡ A 6 4 2
◇ A Q 8 4 3
♣ —

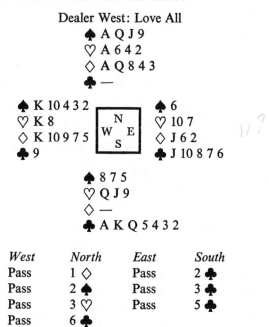

♠ K 10 4 3 2   ♠ 6
♡ K 8   ♡ 10 7
◇ K 10 9 7 5   ◇ J 6 2
♣ 9   ♣ J 10 8 7 6

♠ 8 7 5
♡ Q J 9
◇ —
♣ A K Q 5 4 3 2

West	North	East	South
Pass	1 ◇	Pass	2 ♣
Pass	2 ♠	Pass	3 ♣
Pass	3 ♡	Pass	5 ♣
Pass	6 ♣		

Such was the American sequence. Raising partner's suit with a void is certainly unusual, but Michael Lawrence, North, had a case. Having described the shape of his hand he assumed that Bobby Goldman's clubs were solid. Even if they sprang a small leak, the slam might be there on a finesse, and the Aces were badly in need of points.

Every finesse was right, but the 5–1 trump break, alas, proved fatal. In the other room, the Italians stopped in 5 ♣.

'God must be an Italian,' observed Edgar Kaplan when the match was over.

Mike Lawrence showed his technique in bringing home this grand slam in the semi-finals.

Dealer North: Love All

♠ A Q J
♡ A Q 2
◇ J 9 6 2
♣ A K 2

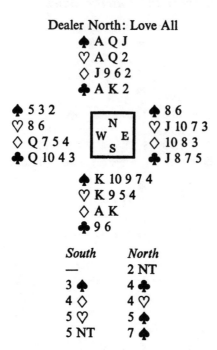

♠ 5 3 2   ♠ 8 6
♡ 8 6   ♡ J 10 7 3
◇ Q 7 5 4   ◇ 10 8 3
♣ Q 10 4 3   ♣ J 8 7 5

♠ K 10 9 7 4
♡ K 9 5 4
◇ A K
♣ 9 6

South	*North*
—	2 NT
3 ♠	4 ♣
4 ◇	4 ♡
5 ♡	5 ♠
5 NT	7 ♠

South's 5 NT is 'Josephine', the grand slam force, named after Josephine Culbertson. This asks partner to bid the grand slam, if he has two of the three top honours in the agreed suit.

West leads the ♠ 3. How should South play?

There are twelve top tricks, thirteen if the hearts break 3–3, or if the ◇ Q comes down. Neither is a good chance and South can do a lot better. After a second round of trumps, to make sure that they are not 4–1, he cashes the ◇ K, crosses to the ♡ A and ruffs a diamond. Going back with a club to the ♣ A, he ruffs a second diamond. Next come the ♣ K and a club ruff. Having scored three tricks by ruffing in his hand, South goes to dummy with a heart and draws the last trump. The ♡ K is his thirteenth trick.

This is how Mike Lawrence played the hand, a perfectly executed dummy reversal.

When your side hasn't bid, and you decide to lead from 9 6 5 2, which card do you choose? It can make all the difference, as on this hand in the Holland-America match.

Dealer West: Love All

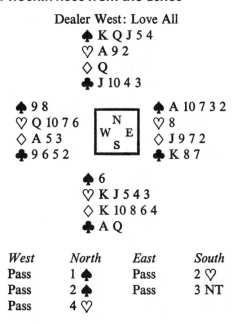

♠ K Q J 5 4
♡ A 9 2
◇ Q
♣ J 10 4 3

♠ 9 8
♡ Q 10 7 6
◇ A 5 3
♣ 9 6 5 2

♠ A 10 7 3 2
♡ 8
◇ J 9 7 2
♣ K 8 7

♠ 6
♡ K J 5 4 3
◇ K 10 8 6 4
♣ A Q

West	North	East	South
Pass	1 ♠	Pass	2 ♡
Pass	2 ♠	Pass	3 NT
Pass	4 ♡		

World champion, Hans Kreyns, West, led the ♣ 2. He would have made the same lead with the ♣ Q, so East went up with the ♣ K, much to the liking of Bobby Wolff, declarer.

Defenders took their two aces, but by now Wolff had more than enough tricks in the side-suits and his only problem was to avoid losing two trumps. In a textbook situation, Wolff didn't falter. He laid down the ♡ K and continued with the ♡ 3, inserting dummy's ♡ 9 when Kreyns played low. Then he cashed his spades. Kreyns ruffed, but with the ♡ A still in dummy, the defence could do no more.

In the other room, against the same contract, Bob Hamman led the ♣ 6 to deny an honour. Soloway, East, played low and declarer was confined to nine tricks.

Though the British failed to reach the semi-finals in the Olympiad, they had the distinction of inflicting a crushing defeat on Italy. The diagrammed hand saw a fascinating battle of wits between Walter Avarelli and Tony Priday.

Dealer North: E/W Vul.

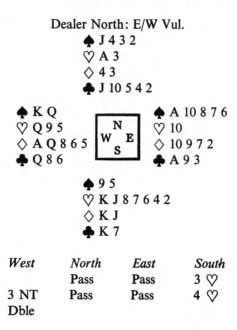

```
                    ♠ J 4 3 2
                    ♡ A 3
                    ◇ 4 3
                    ♣ J 10 5 4 2
♠ K Q                                   ♠ A 10 8 7 6
♡ Q 9 5           ┌─────────┐          ♡ 10
◇ A Q 8 6 5       │    N    │          ◇ 10 9 7 2
♣ Q 8 6          │ W     E │          ♣ A 9 3
                  │    S    │
                  └─────────┘
                    ♠ 9 5
                    ♡ K J 8 7 6 4 2
                    ◇ K J
                    ♣ K 7
```

West	North	East	South
	Pass	Pass	3 ♡
3 NT	Pass	Pass	4 ♡
Dble			

Priday led the ♠ K Q, put Rodrigue in with the ♣ A and won the next two tricks with the ◇ A Q. How should he continue?

Tony led the ♣ Q, one of the best deceptive plays seen in Miami. With malice aforethought, he was presenting declarer with three club tricks.

Turn to Avarelli. Knowing that Priday placed him with the ♡ K J 10, he boldly led the unsupported ♡ J. It held. Next came the ♡ A and it only remained to get back to the ♡ K. Since Tony had persuaded him that he had no more clubs, he tried ruffing a spade, and was duly over-ruffed.

A pretty defence by Tim Seres, one of the world's great card players, cost Britain points in the match against Australia.

Dealer West: Love All

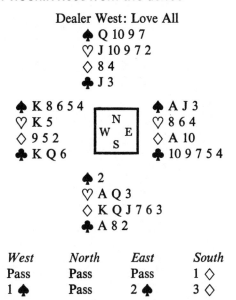

♠ Q 10 9 7
♡ J 10 9 7 2
◊ 8 4
♣ J 3

♠ K 8 6 5 4   ♠ A J 3
♡ K 5   ♡ 8 6 4
◊ 9 5 2   ◊ A 10
♣ K Q 6   ♣ 10 9 7 5 4

♠ 2
♡ A Q 3
◊ K Q J 7 6 3
♣ A 8 2

West	North	East	South
Pass	Pass	Pass	1 ◊
1 ♠	Pass	2 ♣	3 ◊

West leads the ♠ 5. Declarer inserts dummy's ♠ 9 and the ♠ J wins. What card should East play at trick two?

Tim Seres returned the ◊ 10, retaining trump control, yet preventing declarer from ruffing a club in dummy—the nearest approach to having his cake and eating it, too.

Claude Rodrigue, South, led a second trump and now Seres switched to the ♣ 10, proclaiming the ♣ 9 by inference. Winning with the ♣ Q, West had no qualms about continuing with the ♣ K, so setting up a club trick for the defence while he still had the ♡ K.

There was no escape for declarer who had to concede two clubs and a trick in each of the other suits.

Had Seres continued at trick two with the ◊ A and another diamond, Rodrigue would have had time to set up dummy's hearts for club discards.

There was plenty of light relief at Miami to set against the tension of the struggle for world supremacy. The gremlins seem to be unusually active when the great Giorgio Belladonna is at the table, so here he is, sitting South in Italy's match against France.

Dealer South: E/W Vul.

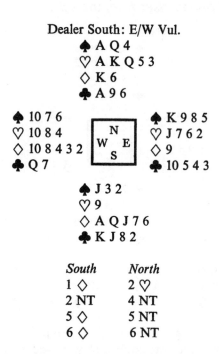

♠ A Q 4
♡ A K Q 5 3
◇ K 6
♣ A 9 6

♠ 10 7 6
♡ 10 8 4
◇ 10 8 4 3 2
♣ Q 7

♠ K 9 8 5
♡ J 7 6 2
◇ 9
♣ 10 5 4 3

♠ J 3 2
♡ 9
◇ A Q J 7 6
♣ K J 8 2

South	North
1 ◇	2 ♡
2 NT	4 NT
5 ◇	5 NT
6 ◇	6 NT

West led a spade, the first trick going to East's ♠ K. The ♠ 5 came back. Winning with the ♠ Q, Belladonna took four diamonds, throwing a club and a heart from the table, and cashed the ♠ A.

To guard his hearts, East had to part with a spade and two clubs, so it only remained for Giorgio to cash his two top clubs to bring down the ♣ Q. Had West been long in hearts, he would have been squeezed in the red suits.

As usual, Belladonna had displayed perfect technique, but the gremlins had the last word. The board, it appears, had strayed from the Ladies Section.

'How could it happen?' the tournament director was asked by the French journalist, José Le Dentu.

'Maybe', replied the director, 'our caddy can't distinguish between men and women.'

Can the lowly four win the first-round trick in a no trump contract? It seems impossible, but it happened in the Switzerland-Peru match.

Dealer South: E/W Vul.

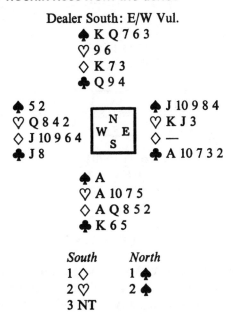

```
              ♠ K Q 7 6 3
              ♡ 9 6
              ◇ K 7 3
              ♣ Q 9 4
  ♠ 5 2                        ♠ J 10 9 8 4
  ♡ Q 8 4 2        N          ♡ K J 3
  ◇ J 10 9 6 4   W   E        ◇ —
  ♣ J 8            S          ♣ A 10 7 3 2
              ♠ A
              ♡ A 10 7 5
              ◇ A Q 8 5 2
              ♣ K 6 5
```

South	*North*
1 ◇	1 ♠
2 ♡	2 ♠
3 NT	

Jean Besse, the Swiss West, led the ♠ 5 to South's ♠ A. A club at trick two was won by East, who promptly switched to the ♡ J, followed by the ♡ K and ♡ 3, West signalling approval.

Winning with the ♡ A, declarer knew that West had the ♡ Q. He had already lost three tricks and his problem was to score four tricks in diamonds without letting in West. So he led the ◇ 2, intending to duck in dummy and put East on play. That would be an insurance against a 4–1 diamond break.

Besse, as he was the first to admit, should have gone up with the ◇ 9, but lazily he followed with the ◇ 4, and since East 'couldn't fail' to overtake, declarer played dummy's ◇ 3.

East showed out and Besse was left holding what he described as 'the cheapest trick of the century'.

The chivalry, so characteristic of Italy's Blue Team, was well illustrated on this hand in the Official Handbook of the Olympiad.

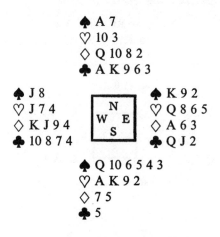

♠ A 7
♡ 10 3
◇ Q 10 8 2
♣ A K 9 6 3

♠ J 8
♡ J 7 4
◇ K J 9 4
♣ 10 8 7 4

♠ K 9 2
♡ Q 8 6 5
◇ A 6 3
♣ Q J 2

♠ Q 10 6 5 4 3
♡ A K 9 2
◇ 7 5
♣ 5

CONTRACT 4 ♠: LEAD ♣ 4

Going up with the ♣ A, Walter Avarelli, South, threw the ◇ 5 on the ♣ K, cashed the ♡ A K and ruffed a heart. A club ruff and a heart, ruffed with the ♠ A, and another club ruff followed. Then came a low spade to West's ♠ 8, the ◇ A and ◇ 6 ruffed by Avarelli.

Two cards remained and he had lost two tricks. With the ♠ K J 9 still out, he sat with ♠ Q 10. Which should he play? Looking for inspiration, he faced the ♠ 5, the last card he had played—the traditional non-verbal request to see the previous trick.

Misunderstanding, East faced the ♠ J. Avarelli refused to take advantage of an exposed card and shuffling his two cards, face downwards, he invited East, then West, to pick one. When both refused, he called on a bystander who chose the ♠ Q, scooping the ♠ J and setting up Avarelli's ♠ 10 as his tenth trick.

Why did Avarelli use sign language?

His English, explains the Official Handbook, isn't as good as his bridge.

Outgunned in Miami, and again in the World Championship of 1973 at Guaruja, the Aces had the consolation of seeing their top pair, Bobby Wolff and Bob Hamman win the World Olympiad Pairs in Las Palmas. This hand was a good illustration of match-point psychology.

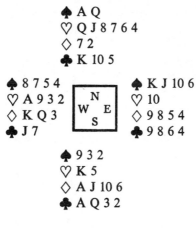

      ♠ A Q
      ♡ Q J 8 7 6 4
      ◇ 7 2
      ♣ K 10 5

♠ 8 7 5 4   ♠ K J 10 6
♡ A 9 3 2   N   ♡ 10
◇ K Q 3   W   E   ◇ 9 8 5 4
♣ J 7   S   ♣ 9 8 6 4

      ♠ 9 3 2
      ♡ K 5
      ◇ A J 10 6
      ♣ A Q 3 2

CONTRACT 3 NT: LEAD ♠ 8

I don't know the bidding, but the contract is clearly a poor one, especially played by South.

Bobby Wolff, who was declarer, lost the ♠ Q to East's ♠ K and was in dummy at trick two with the ♠ A. A heart to the king and ace was followed by two more spades, then by a diamond, won by the ◇ A.

How should Bobby Wolff play?

He had noted, of course, East's ♡ 10, but was it bare or was it a false card?

Bobby led the ♡ 5—and finessed the ♡ 6! He reasoned that if hearts broke 3–2, all the North-South pairs in 4 ♡ would easily make game, and since, come what may, he couldn't make ten tricks in no trumps, he would score a near-bottom.

The only hope was a bad heart break. Then, at least, some of the pairs in the superior 4 ♡ contract would fail—which is what happened.

Straight from Las Palmas the newly-crowned World Pairs champions flew to Venice for the Bermuda Bowl match of 1974.

Three of the *squadra azzurra*'s veterans had bowed out, and with Bianchi, de Falco and Franco replacing Avarelli, D'Alelio and Pabis-Ticci, the Aces nearly brought it off.

At one point, a mere 5 IMPs separated the two sides and with only thirteen boards to go it was anyone's match. Then came this dramatic deal which virtually settled the issue.

```
        ♠ K 2              ┌──────┐    ♠ A Q 10 8 5
        ♡ 10 5 3          │   N  │    ♡ A 9
        ◇ A K Q 5         │ W  E │    ◇ 2
        ♣ J 10 9 8        │   S  │    ♣ A Q 5 3 2
                          └──────┘
```

With Bobby Wolff, West, and Bob Hamman, East, the Blue Club sequence was:

Wolff	*Hamman*
1 ◇	2 ♣
2 NT	3 ♠
4 ♠	

On the system, Hamman's reverse showed strength and long spades, but it didn't promise a club suit. That he had one was purely incidental, so Wolff never came to support clubs.

Now for the smooth Precision bidding of Forquet and Bianchi.

Forquet	*Bianchi*
1 ◇	1 ♠
1 NT	3 ♣
3 ◇	3 ♡
4 ♣	4 ◇
4 ♠	6 ♣

So natural was this sequence that it might well have been Acol as practised by the moderns. Forquet's 3 ◇ was an advance cue-bid. Bianchi showed the ♡ A and Pietro Forquet, after confirming clubs, showed the ♠ K. Following his 1 NT rebid, the second round control couldn't be a singleton, as was Bianchi's 4 ◇. Having exchanged exact pictures of the two hands, the Italians bid a perfect slam—and gained 12 IMPs at a critical state of the World Championship.

Venice was memorable for the introduction of screens, placed diagonally between the players, so as to render partner and **one** of the opponents invisible. Combined with bidding boxes this should have precluded any possibility of conveying improper information.

Alas, despite all these security measures, a storm broke out the following year in Bermuda, where the 1975 World Championship was held twenty-five years after its inauguration.

If facial expressions and tell-tale pauses were ruled out, there was nothing to prevent freedom of manoeuvre, under the table, and the Italians, Facchini and Zuchelli, were roundly accused of foot-tapping.

The ensuing melodrama, with no heroes and America's captain, Alfred Sheinwold, as the big bad wolf, stole the limelight from the bridge.

The Italians won, but everything about the finals, except the outcome, confounded expectations.

Tense and overwrought, unnerved by the accusations against their team-mates, Giorgio and Benito showed little of their customary artistry as they went to do battle with the Americans, who had only narrowly beaten France in the semi-finals.

From the first, everything went in favour of the Americans. After board 51 they were in front by no less than 77 IMPs—143 to 66—a lead described by several correspondents as 'insurmountable'. The American camp was jubilant.

This was one of the many swings against Italy.

Dealer South: E/W Vul.

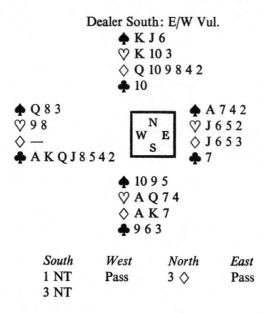

South	West	North	East
South	*West*	*North*	*East*
1 NT	Pass	3 ◊	Pass
3 NT			

West was Billy Eisenberg, one of the original Dallas Aces. His well-judged pass brought its own reward when Garozzo, South, rebid 3 NT over Belladonna's 3 ◊.

Passing again with alacrity, Billy led the ♣ J, his 'fourth' highest, and the defence collected the first nine tricks.

Observe that had Billy doubled, opponents might have retreated into diamonds and as the cards lie, they would make eleven tricks.

In the other room, West didn't show the same self-restraint and went one down in 4 ♣.

At Waterloo, Napoleon sighed in vain for the sun of Austerlitz. But there was to be no Waterloo for the Italians. The blazing sun of Austerlitz came out in all its glory, and sweeping all before them, they drew level, then forged ahead.

When board 92, surely destined to remain forever the most spectacular hand in the history of the Bowl, was placed on the table, Italy was 13 IMPs in front.

Dealer East: N/S Vul.

♠ Q J 8
♡ A J 9 6 5
◇ K 8 2
♣ A Q

♠ 7 6 5 2   ♠ 4 3
♡ K 4 3 2   ♡ Q 10 8 7
◇ J 5 3   ◇ Q 10 6 4
♣ K 10   ♣ 7 5 4

♠ A K 10 9
♡ —
◇ A 9 7
♣ J 9 8 6 3 2

The Americans bid and made 6 NT.

Belladonna and Garozzo, after a sequence of fourteen bids, ended in 7 ♣.

An audience of 700, watching the drama on closed circuit TV, saw Giorgio's mobile features register a series of emotions. First, as dummy went down, acute dismay, then hope when he saw the ♣ 10 appear at trick two, followed by suspense as he waited for Billy Eisenberg to play to dummy's ♣ Q. Was Edwin Kantar's ♣ 10 a true card? Would the ♣ K really drop on the ♣ A?

When it did, Belladonna, a devout Catholic, quickly crossed himself. His face was wreathed in smiles.

The grand slam was made and Italy retained the Bowl. And yet, even with so lucky a distribution, the contract might have been defeated.

As several experts were quick to point out, Kantar had everything to gain and nothing to lose by going up with the ♣ K at once. If the ♣ K were bare, the grand slam could still be made. Declarer would shorten his trumps by ruffing two hearts, cash two diamonds and three spades, and with the lead in his hand, bring about this position.

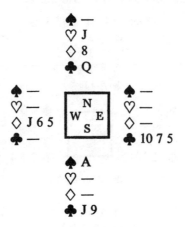

The ♠ A is ruffed and East is helpless.

Had Belladonna believed Kantar he would have gone down if, that is, Kantar had played the ♣ K. And then the Bermuda Bowl would have been won by America—by 3 IMPs!

SECOND INTERVAL
A visit to my coven
facts, files and fiction

The curtain comes down on Act II.

As the actors leave the stage, I invite the reader to come with me behind the scenes and learn the secrets of my trade.

The coven, wherein I mix my potions, is close by, next to the dressing-room, and from time to time the actors come over to watch me mix the brew. Let's make it a party.

How should a writer set out to bewitch his readers?

The first step is to look into a crystal and discover what they want. That's better, by far, than studying their letters, for readers write only to bury Caesar, not to praise him, and if they find nothing wrong with his column, they do not write at all, caring little whether Caesar is dead or alive.

A reliable crystal will soon reveal that the average reader wants to learn, so long as he can do it the easy way. He is avid for knowledge, if he can acquire it painlessly, not otherwise. So instruction must slither smoothly down his gullet and never be rammed down his throat.

Quizzes and problems go down well, but they mustn't be too difficult and solutions should always be close at hand. Stimulation, without frustration, should be the objective.

Monotony, though not listed in the top seven, is the deadliest of all sins and the bridge writer should never forget that on paper every South looks much alike and so does West and East, and even North, the lowly dummy. To bring the cardinal points to life he should give them flesh and blood and the contours of Omar or Slavenburg or Rixi.

An uppercut by Belladonna in a big money tournament in Monte Carlo or a dummy reversal by Billy Eisenberg at the World Championship in Rio is more vibrant, and therefore more instructive than the same play by a symbol presiding over a diagram.

Personality pieces usually make good journalism, but they mustn't be too contrived. Ghost writers have been respectable, even fashionable, for years, so presumably readers believe that the celebrities whose names they see at the top of the column really write—or read—the contents. But ghost declarers would strain their credulity too much. The journalist must stick to genuine characters. If, as in the case of Omar Sharif, hearts flutter and bosoms heave, so much the better, but it would be no good foisting a smother play on Sophia Loren or a suicide squeeze on Wedgwood Benn. Wishful thinking should never be carried too far.

The crystal has told us enough. As I put it away and open the door of my coven, rows of shelves come into view, stocked with bridge books of every size and colour, bound volumes of magazines, British and American, stacks of *Le Bridgeur*, piles of *Bridge d'Italia*, and many other publications from the world over.

That library, always growing, always kept up to date, provides me with the bulk of my raw material. For the rest I look to classified files with cuttings and clippings and notes on hands that I have come across in play.

My library never lets me down.

A big event is coming up, say the European Championship, and I want to enliven my column with a topical piece about some of the stars taking part. I pick up a back number or two and before long this appears in my daily column.

'No players at the European Championship are more popular than the Spaniards. If their skill equalled their old-world courtesy, they would be invincible. Though rarely among the leaders in international events, the Spanish team includes some fine card players. Here is one of their stars, Jaime Dezcallar, in action against Finland, at Estoril, in 1970.

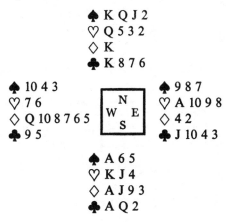

```
              ♠ K Q J 2
              ♡ Q 5 3 2
              ◇ K
              ♣ K 8 7 6
♠ 10 4 3                      ♠ 9 8 7
♡ 7 6              N          ♡ A 10 9 8
◇ Q 10 8 7 6 5  W   E         ◇ 4 2
♣ 9 5              S          ♣ J 10 4 3
              ♠ A 6 5
              ♡ K J 4
              ◇ A J 9 3
              ♣ A Q 2
```

CONTRACT 6 NT: LEAD ♣ 9

'Winning with the ♣ A, Dezcallar crossed to dummy with a spade to lead a heart to his ♡ K, which held. Then he repeated the process and when the ♡ J scored, too, a picture of the deal began to come into view.

'Unless East had four hearts, would he have held up his ♡ A twice? And what was West's ♣ 9 with nothing better than the ♣ 5 behind it? Surely a doubleton. If so, neither the hearts nor the clubs would break, but since West was short in both, he must be long in diamonds.

'Jaime Dezcallar took the spades, throwing his last heart, and cashed the ◇ K, then the ♣ K. Giving up all hope of a fourth trick in clubs, he came to hand with the ♣ Q and exited with the ◇ 9, forcing a diamond from West into his ◇ A J.'

Or maybe trials are being held to select the British team. I have a choice of hands and pick this one.

Dealer South: Game All

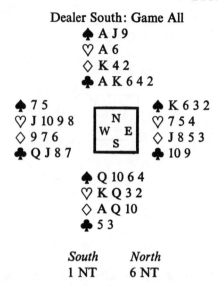

♠ A J 9
♡ A 6
◇ K 4 2
♣ A K 6 4 2

♠ 7 5
♡ J 10 9 8
◇ 9 7 6
♣ Q J 8 7

♠ K 6 3 2
♡ 7 5 4
◇ J 8 5 3
♣ 10 9

♠ Q 10 6 4
♡ K Q 3 2
◇ A Q 10
♣ 5 3

South	North
1 NT	6 NT

North-South are Tony Priday and Claude Rodrigue.

Rodrigue had the routine weak no trump which this pair play, regardless of vulnerability. Priday's tops and and five-card suit were worth a point or two, so he jumped straight to 6 NT.

On the lead of the ♡ J, what is the correct play? If the clubs split 3–3 declarer will still need the spade finesse. So which suit should he try first? Or doesn't it matter?

In fact, it makes all the difference, because if the spade finesse fails, declarer can't afford to give up a club. At trick two, Rodrigue duly finessed the spade, losing to East's ♠ K. A heart came back. Was any hope left?

One chance remained—to find the same defender guarding both hearts and clubs. After four spades, two hearts and three diamonds, West was down to four cards and he had to keep five—two hearts and three clubs. The ♡ 2 or the ♣ 2 was destined to score the twelfth trick.

I hear that Jim Borin will be coming over shortly from Melbourne to visit his parents. With his wife, Norma, he will be playing for Australia in Taipeh, the first husband and wife combination to represent their country for a long, long time. So for a

topical hand I turn to *Australian Bridge,* and I soon find the
Borins playing for Victoria against New South Wales.

Dealer East: Love All

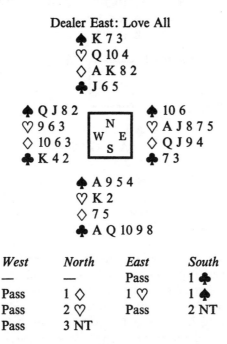

♠ K 7 3
♡ Q 10 4
◇ A K 8 2
♣ J 6 5

♠ Q J 8 2
♡ 9 6 3
◇ 10 6 3
♣ K 4 2

♠ 10 6
♡ A J 8 7 5
◇ Q J 9 4
♣ 7 3

♠ A 9 5 4
♡ K 2
◇ 7 5
♣ A Q 10 9 8

West	North	East	South
—	—	Pass	1 ♣
Pass	1 ◇	1 ♡	1 ♠
Pass	2 ♡	Pass	2 NT
Pass	3 NT		

West led the ♡ 9. How would a knowledgeable kibitzer view
the prospects? The contract, he would say, is unmakeable. The
♡ K is driven out at once, and since West comes in with the ♣ K,
a second heart through dummy yields the defence four more
tricks.

And yet, by subtle deception, Jim Borin made the contract. At
trick one, he went up with dummy's ♡ Q! This is the classical
play when declarer holds K x x. Now East must wait for West to
lead the suit again. Otherwise he loses a trick for nothing.

Assuming that Borin had a third heart, East switched—and
lived to regret it.

In the same issue of *Australian Bridge* I find a brilliant display
by Tim Seres.

Dealer West: Love All

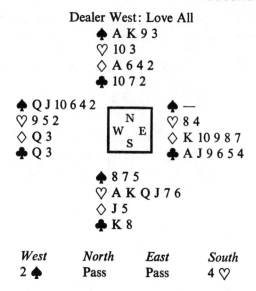

♠ A K 9 3
♡ 10 3
◇ A 6 4 2
♣ 10 7 2

♠ Q J 10 6 4 2
♡ 9 5 2
◇ Q 3
♣ Q 3

♠ —
♡ 8 4
◇ K 10 9 8 7
♣ A J 9 6 5 4

♠ 8 7 5
♡ A K Q J 7 6
◇ J 5
♣ K 8

West	*North*	*East*	*South*
2 ♠	Pass	Pass	4 ♡

West led the ♠ Q. Declarer appears to have four inescapable losers—a spade ruff, another spade, a diamond and a club.

After studying dummy for fully ten seconds, a long time for him, Tim Seres played low! Thereafter he couldn't be defeated. West continued with the ♠ J covered by the ♠ K and ruffed. East returned a diamond to dummy's ◇ A, but Seres was now in command. He drew trumps, took the marked finesse against the ♠ 10 and discarded his losing diamond on the ♠ A.

Had West switched to a diamond at trick two, it wouldn't have helped. After drawing trumps, Seres would have led a spade, forcing West to split his ♠ J 10. Later he would have finessed against the remaining honour, conceding only the first spade trick, one diamond and one club.

The contract is unmakeable if the ♠ Q is covered at trick one.

Soon the *Sunday Times* Pairs will be upon us and I look for a personality piece to coincide with the event. No one can suit me better than that gay buccaneer, Bob Slavenburg. Going through my records, I soon find this characteristic Slavenburg performance in the Holland-Ireland match in the European Championship at Estoril.

Dealer North: E/W Vul.

♠ A Q 6 4
♡ Q 4
◇ K 5 2
♣ K 9 5 2

♠ 9 8 2
♡ K 9 7 3
◇ 9 6 4
♣ A Q 3

♠ J 10 7 5 3
♡ J 8 6 5
◇ 7
♣ J 7 6

♠ K
♡ A 10 2
◇ A Q J 10 8 3
♣ 10 8 4

Hans Kreyns, sitting North, dealt and opened 1 ♣. Slavenburg, South, forced with 2 ◇, rebid diamonds, and, after checking aces, finished in 6 ◇. A speculative contract, to say the least, but not more so than many others which Slavenburg has brought home.

The lead was a trump, taken by Slavenburg in the closed hand. Playing with his usual speed—in marked contrast to some of the other competitors—he led a club, going up with the ♣ K when West played low. Next he laid down the ◇ A, cashed the ♠ K, crossed to dummy with the ◇ K and parked his two club losers on the ♠ A Q. All that now remained was to get back with a spade ruff and lead a heart to dummy's ♡ Q. West scored the ♡ K and no more.

Most of our leading players, as well as visiting celebrities from abroad, are to be found daily at the Eccentric Club, where I play three or four times a week.

I sat West on this deal:

Dealer South: Love All

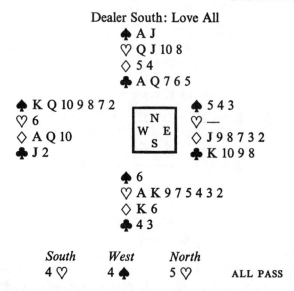

South	West	North	
4 ♡	4 ♠	5 ♡	ALL PASS

As I led the ♠ K and dummy came into view, the kibitzers exchanged knowing looks. A player, waiting to cut in, glanced unobtrusively at my cards and walked to another table. Clearly, with both the ◇ A and ♣ K badly placed, the rubber wouldn't be over that hand.

How would the reader plan the play? As he ponders, he may be comforted by the thought that ninety-nine declarers out of a hundred would go down.

Sitting South was Irving Rose, one of Britain's best dummy players, and he made the contract before touching a single card in his hand! On my ♠ K he threw dummy's ♠ J. That was the key play. I switched to a trump, but it made no difference. Rose had reason to place me with the ♣ K, of course, since I had bid 4 ♠, but he wasn't concerned with finesses. On the ♠ A he threw a club. Then he laid down the ♣ A and ruffed a club. Crossing to the table twice with trumps, he ruffed two more clubs and he still had a trump entry to get at the fifth club, his eleventh trick.

As the cards lie, we can, of course, make 5 ♠.

Here's another hand from the Eccentric, starring Claude Rodrigue.

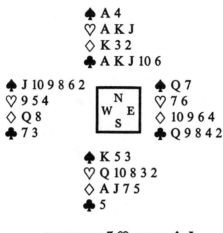

♠ A 4
♡ A K J
◇ K 3 2
♣ A K J 10 6

♠ J 10 9 8 6 2
♡ 9 5 4
◇ Q 8
♣ 7 3

♠ Q 7
♡ 7 6
◇ 10 9 6 4
♣ Q 9 8 4 2

♠ K 5 3
♡ Q 10 8 3 2
◇ A J 7 5
♣ 5

CONTRACT 7 ♡: LEAD ♠ J

There are twelve top tricks, including a spade ruff in dummy, and declarer looks to the clubs for the thirteenth.

First Rodrigue tested trumps. When both opponents followed, he laid down the ♣ A and ruffed a club. After two rounds of spades and a spade ruff, he ruffed a club high and drew the outstanding trump.

Dummy's last four cards were ◇ K 2 and ♣ K J, while declarer retained the ◇ A J 7 5. Crossing to the ◇ K, Rodrigue cashed the ♣ K and led the ◇ 2, East following with the ◇ 4. Claude promptly went up with the ◇ A and dropped West's ◇ Q.

Why didn't he finesse? That appears to be the correct play, and yet dropping the ◇ Q was a certainty. East's last card was known to be the ♣ Q, so he couldn't have the ◇ Q.

No one has been more helpful to me over the years than Claude. Always at the hub of things, he has an uncanny memory for hands, and what's more, he writes them down legibly. This was one from Britain's match against Israel at Ostend in the European Championship of 1973. On the result of the hand depended the outcome of the match.

Dealer North: E/W Vul.

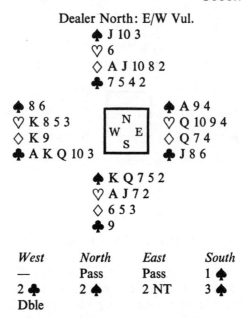

	West	North	East	South
	—	Pass	Pass	1 ♠
	2 ♣	2 ♠	2 NT	3 ♠
	Dble			

West leads the ♣ K and switches to a trump, ducked by East. How can South conjure up nine tricks?

Winning in his hand, Rodrigue led a diamond, taking West's ◇ K with dummy's ◇ A. East won the next diamond trick and gave his partner a diamond ruff. Now came the ♣ A. The defence had taken three tricks. Claude ruffed, cashed his ♡ A and ruffed a heart in dummy. Now the stage was set for a coup.

On two good diamonds in dummy, Claude could throw two losing hearts. So East had to ruff. Over-ruffing, Rodrigue ruffed a heart with dummy's last trump and led another diamond.

Whether or not East ruffed with his ♠ A, Rodrigue would shed a heart—and make his contract.

The 1972 Olympiad in Miami, which we kibitzed during Act II, was the scene of another Rodrigue hand which I presented in the *Evening Standard* as a quiz.

Dealer South: Both Vul.

♠ K 5 2
♡ J 9
◇ K Q 2
♣ K J 7 4 2

♠ A Q J 8 4
♡ A K 7
◇ 10
♣ A 10 9 6

South	North
1 ♠	2 ♣
3 ♡	4 ♠
6 ♠	

It's by no means a difficult slam to reach, but how should South play? West leads the ◇ 6.

West's lead transforms the situation. No sane defender would underlead an ace against a slam after the bidding sequence shown above. Of course, declarer can set up a certain diamond trick by going up with an honour, but one discard would be useless to him. He needs two, if he is to be spared the guess in clubs.

South should, therefore, play low from dummy in the hope that West led from the ◇ J. He has everything to gain and nothing to lose.

♠ 10 9 3   ♠ 7 6
♡ 10 8 5   ♡ Q 6 4 3 2
◇ J 9 7 6   ◇ A 8 5 4 3
♣ Q 8 5   ♣ 3

And that's how Claude Rodrigue played the hand in America. Omar Sharif is the bridge columnist's best friend. If he is short of material, Omar will provide him with it, for never shall it be said of him: 'Full many a flower is born to blush unseen, And waste its sweetness on the desert air.'

Every hand that Omar plays, every bid, every coup is taken down and used in evidence in his favour. No issue of *Le Bridgeur* or *Bridge de France* goes out without some reference to Omar.

He is South on both the hands that follow:

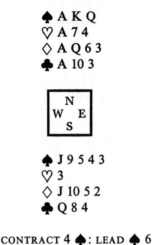

♠ A K Q
♡ A 7 4
◇ A Q 6 3
♣ A 10 3

```
    N
W       E
    S
```

♠ J 9 5 4 3
♡ 3
◇ J 10 5 2
♣ Q 8 4

CONTRACT 4 ♠ : LEAD ♠ 6

On the second round of trumps, West discarded the ♡ 9. Can Omar make the contract?

Ten tricks are there—five trumps, three diamonds and two aces. The snag is that declarer can only get to his hand to draw trumps by ruffing a heart, and if he does that, he will have no trump left to stop the hearts which opponents will surely unleash when they come in with a diamond.

Omar Sharif found a neat solution. After cashing dummy's three top spades, he led a low heart. No matter what opponents did next, Omar was in control. With the ♡ A still in dummy, he could afford to ruff a heart, leave himself without a trump, and set up the diamonds.

The East-West hands were:

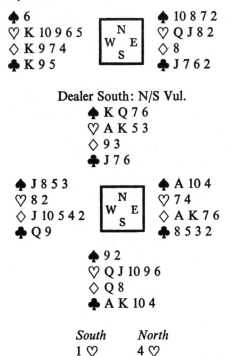

♠ 6
♡ K 10 9 6 5
◇ K 9 7 4
♣ K 9 5

♠ 10 8 7 2
♡ Q J 8 2
◇ 8
♣ J 7 6 2

Dealer South: N/S Vul.

♠ K Q 7 6
♡ A K 5 3
◇ 9 3
♣ J 7 6

♠ J 8 5 3
♡ 8 2
◇ J 10 5 4 2
♣ Q 9

♠ A 10 4
♡ 7 4
◇ A K 7 6
♣ 8 5 3 2

♠ 9 2
♡ Q J 10 9 6
◇ Q 8
♣ A K 10 4

South	North
1 ♡	4 ♡

West led the ♠ 3. Capturing dummy's ♠ Q with the ♠ A, East laid down the ◇ K and continued with the ♣ 5. How should Omar play?

All appears to depend on the club finesse, which is destined to fail. Neatly side-stepping destiny, Omar Sharif made his contract. Going up with the ♣ A, he led a spade to the ♠ K and ruffed a spade. Then he crossed to dummy's ♡ A and ruffed the last spade. Next he played the ♡ K and ♣ K, dropping West's ♣ Q. Was that lucky? Not entirely. East's ♣ 5 was a deceptive card, but it told Omar that he didn't have the ♣ Q. Otherwise he would have surely cashed his ◇ A and exited with a spade. Why play away from the ♣ Q?

Had the ♣ Q not dropped, Omar would have exited with the ◇ Q to East's ◇ A. East might have started with two clubs only, in which case he would have been obliged to concede a ruff and discard.

Rixi and Fritzi are almost as prolific a source of material for the bridge writer as Omar Sharif. Again, it isn't only because they play so well, but because everyone always knows all about it.

Commenting on their overwhelming victory in the Ladies Pairs in the 1974 Olympiad, French international, José Le Dentu wrote in *Le Figaro*: 'Their superiority lies as much in simple, direct, aggressive bidding as in a gift for card play equal to that of the men.' And he selected this hand as typical of the style of the two 'superstars'.

Dealer East: N/S Vul.

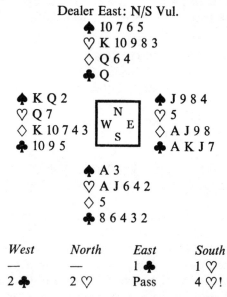

```
              ♠ 10 7 6 5
              ♡ K 10 9 8 3
              ◇ Q 6 4
              ♣ Q

♠ K Q 2            N            ♠ J 9 8 4
♡ Q 7         W       E        ♡ 5
◇ K 10 7 4 3       S           ◇ A J 9 8
♣ 10 9 5                       ♣ A K J 7

              ♠ A 3
              ♡ A J 6 4 2
              ◇ 5
              ♣ 8 6 4 3 2
```

West	North	East	South
—	—	1 ♣	1 ♡
2 ♣	2 ♡	Pass	4 ♡!

The jump to 4 ♡ by Rixi, who was South, appears to be fool-hardy. And yet it was based on simple logic. Fritzi could have at most one club, and since she had no other suit to bid, she might have five hearts. That would only leave three losers. Besides a bold jump to 4 ♡ might drive opponents into a costly 5 ♣.

Rixi's calculations proved correct. She ruffed three clubs in dummy, to set up her fifth club and scored ten tricks, with one spade, five hearts, three club ruffs and a club—ten tricks out of thirteen with sixteen points against twenty-four!

Henri Svarc and Jean-Michel Boulenger, one of the best pairs in the world during the past decade, were the victims of typical strong-arm tactics by Rixi in the *Sunday Times* Pairs.

Dealer West: Both Vul.

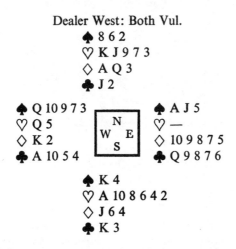

```
              ♠ 8 6 2
              ♡ K J 9 7 3
              ◇ A Q 3
              ♣ J 2

♠ Q 10 9 7 3        ♠ A J 5
♡ Q 5         N      ♡ —
◇ K 2      W     E   ◇ 10 9 8 7 5
♣ A 10 5 4     S     ♣ Q 9 8 7 6

              ♠ K 4
              ♡ A 10 8 6 4 2
              ◇ J 6 4
              ♣ K 3
```

Most Wests opened 1 ♠ and most Souths played in 4 ♡, scoring 620. When Fritzi Gordon, North, and Rixi Markus, South, opposed the Frenchmen, the bidding took an unexpected turn.

West	North	East	South
1 ♠	2 ♡	2 ♠	3 NT!

Svarc, East, doubled, and Rixi stuck it manfully, of course. A spade was led, not that the lead mattered, and Rixi Markus quickly wrapped up ten tricks to score 950, a clear top.

'I had to protect my kings,' she said simply when asked why she bid 3 NT and not 4 ♡.

The reasoning is sound. Not only is it easier to make nine tricks than ten, but with 1 ♠ bid by West, there is everything to be said for steering the contract into South's hand. Why didn't any other South think of it?

An example of Svarc's technique is this *Scissors Coup* against the Blue Team at Rio in 1969, the last World Championship won by the *squadra azzurra* before they retired—that is, the first time.

Dealer South: Love All

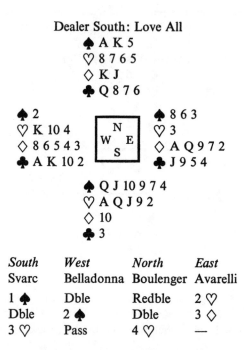

♠ A K 5
♡ 8 7 6 5
◇ K J
♣ Q 8 7 6

♠ 2   ♠ 8 6 3
♡ K 10 4   ♡ 3
◇ 8 6 5 4 3   ◇ A Q 9 7 2
♣ A K 10 2   ♣ J 9 5 4

♠ Q J 10 9 7 4
♡ A Q J 9 2
◇ 10
♣ 3

South	West	North	East
Svarc	Belladonna	Boulenger	Avarelli
1 ♠	Dble	Redble	2 ♡
Dble	2 ♠	Dble	3 ◇
3 ♡	Pass	4 ♡	—

The Roman bidding system seems puzzling at first. The key is Avarelli's 2 ♡ response to the take-out double. It shows his *shortest suit*. Then, in answer to 2 ♠, he chooses between the minors.

Belladonna led the ♣ K and switched to the ♠ 2, unmistakeably a singleton. Believing, with good reason, that the trump finesse would fail, how should Svarc continue? To play the ♡ A, then the ♡ Q, won't help if West has a third heart and finds East with the ◇ A—which, of course, is what would happen.

Svarc led dummy's ♣ Q and threw on it his ◇ 10—the *Scissors Coup*. Having cut communications between defenders, Svarc was safe. The ruff could no longer materialize.

In the other room, East-West didn't bid, and without the take-out double to help him, Forquet went down in 4 ♡.

What happens when Greek meets Greek, or rather when Italian meets Italian?

Asked for a hand which had given him special pleasure, Belladonna picked this one from rubber bridge:

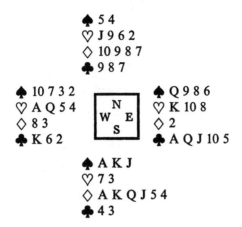

```
              ♠ 5 4
              ♡ J 9 6 2
              ◇ 10 9 8 7
              ♣ 9 8 7
  ♠ 10 7 3 2            ♠ Q 9 8 6
  ♡ A Q 5 4      N      ♡ K 10 8
  ◇ 8 3       W   E     ◇ 2
  ♣ K 6 2        S      ♣ A Q J 10 5
              ♠ A K J
              ♡ 7 3
              ◇ A K Q J 5 4
              ♣ 4 3
```

Sitting South, Belladonna doubled East's 4 ♠ and led out the two top diamonds. East ruffed and played a low trump towards the table. Concealing his knave, Belladonna won with the ♠ A and continued with a third diamond. Declarer ruffed in dummy and led another trump, intending to take the 'marked' finesse against North's knave. After that he could claim the contract. The sudden appearance of the ♠ J in South's hand came as a horrible surprise. Belladonna drew trumps and cashed three more diamonds. Four down.

Who was East? None other than Belladonna's close friend and partner, Benito Garozzo.

One of my most valuable files houses the International Bridge Press Association's *Bulletin*, brilliantly edited by Albert Dormer. All the best-known bridge writers take the *Bulletin* and most of them contribute to it as well, reporting hands of interest from the four corners of the world.

Not the least of the attractions of the *Bulletin* is the inclusion in every issue of four deals by the famous Swedish analyst, Jan Wohlin. This hand is typical—simple and straightforward, yet far from easy.

Dealer West: Both Vul.

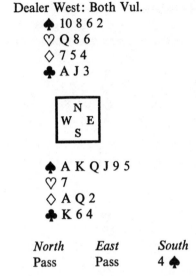

♠ 10 8 6 2
♡ Q 8 6
◇ 7 5 4
♣ A J 3

♠ A K Q J 9 5
♡ 7
◇ A Q 2
♣ K 6 4

West	North	East	South
1 ♡	Pass	Pass	4 ♠

West leads the ♡ K and switches to the ♣ 10. How should South play?

If he inserts the ♣ J, East covers with the ♣ Q. South can ruff out the hearts and exit with a club, but West will unblock and East will lead a diamond through the ◇ A Q.

Can East be kept out of the lead?

Yes, and all South need do to bring home his contract is to let West hold the ♣ 10!

♠ —   ♠ 7 4 3
♡ A K J 9 5 3   ♡ 10 4 2
◇ K 10 6 3   ◇ J 9 8
♣ 10 9 5   ♣ Q 8 7 2

No matter what West does next, declarer will draw trumps, ruff a heart, cash the ♣ K, then the ♣ A and lead dummy's ♡ Q, discarding the ◇ 2.

West, who was effectively end-played at trick two, must either concede a ruff and discard or lead away from his ♦ K.

Here's another Wohlin hand.

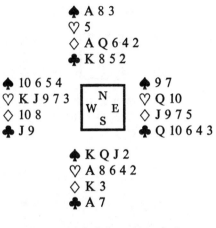

```
              ♠ A 8 3
              ♡ 5
              ♦ A Q 6 4 2
              ♣ K 8 5 2

    ♠ 10 6 5 4                    ♠ 9 7
    ♡ K J 9 7 3    N             ♡ Q 10
    ♦ 10 8      W     E          ♦ J 9 7 5
    ♣ J 9          S             ♣ Q 10 6 4 3

              ♠ K Q J 2
              ♡ A 8 6 4 2
              ♦ K 3
              ♣ A 7
```

CONTRACT 6 ♠ : LEAD ♠ 4

South has ten top tricks, four trumps, the ♡ A, the ♦ A K Q and the ♣ A K. Needing two more, he wins the first trick with the ♠ A and sets out to ruff two hearts in dummy. This is the natural line of play and most of the time it will succeed. Occasionally, however, the distribution will be unkind, as above, and a defender will over-ruff the third round of hearts.

Unlucky? Certainly, but declarer can guard against it. Expecting the spades and diamonds to break 4–2, in accordance with the odds, he plays a low diamond from both hands at trick two. Now, unless the trumps or diamonds are 5–1, all is well. A trump return is the best defence, but it doesn't worry South. He wins, ruffs a heart, comes to hand with the ♣ A, draws trumps, cashes the ♦ K and crosses to dummy with the ♣ K to score three good diamonds.

On the last day of the week I present my readers with a quiz. Wohlin has often given me ideas, as here:

Dealer South: Love All

♠ 9 5 2
♡ A 6
♢ A K 6 2
♣ Q 7 4 3

```
    N
  W   E
    S
```

♠ A K 6 4 3
♡ K Q J 10 9 5
♢ 7 3
♣ —

South	*North*
2 ♡	3 ♢
3 ♠	5 ♡
6 ♣	6 ♢
6 ♡	

West leads the ♢ Q. How should South plan the play?

Since only a bad spade break can prove embarrassing, declarer should give it his undivided attention. At trick two he leads a spade to his ♠ A, crosses to dummy with a diamond and leads another spade. So long as West doesn't ruff, nothing can go wrong. Declarer concedes a spade, ruffs another with the ♡ A and sets up his last spade.

♠ Q 10 8 7   ♠ J
♡ 8 4 3   ♡ 7 2
♢ Q J 10   ♢ 9 8 5 4
♣ K J 9   ♣ A 10 8 6 5 2

```
    N
  W   E
    S
```

Should East ruff the second spade, it would do him no good. South would lay down the ♡ K—removing East's second trump —cash the ♠ K and ruff as before.

Had West opened a trump, as he should have done on the bidding, South would have stood no chance.

Wohlin hands provided me with the material for *Best of Bridge*, which I wrote in collaboration with Eric Jannersten. Eric and Jan once played together for Sweden. Here they are in a European Championship.

Dealer West: E/W Vul.

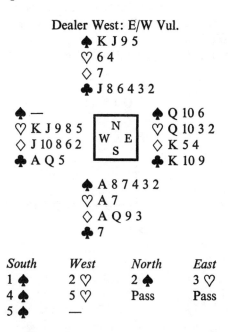

♠ K J 9 5
♡ 6 4
◇ 7
♣ J 8 6 4 3 2

♠ —
♡ K J 9 8 5
◇ J 10 8 6 2
♣ A Q 5

♠ Q 10 6
♡ Q 10 3 2
◇ K 5 4
♣ K 10 9

♠ A 8 7 4 3 2
♡ A 7
◇ A Q 9 3
♣ 7

South	West	North	East
1 ♠	2 ♡	2 ♠	3 ♡
4 ♠	5 ♡	Pass	Pass
5 ♠	—		

Jannersten, West, led the ♡ 8 to the queen and ace. Declarer crossed to dummy with the ♠ K, led the ◇ 7, finessed successfully and threw dummy's heart on the ◇ A. Next he ruffed a heart and led a club, Wohlin's ♣ 9 holding the trick. What should Wohlin do now?

On the bidding, South can have no more hearts, and the play shows that his club was a singleton. So he started with four diamonds and can make his contract by ruffing two diamonds and conceding a trump. By leading the ♠ 10 East can stop a diamond ruff at the cost of a trump trick. But the ♠ Q, leaving the ♠ J as dummy's only trump, prevents South from ruffing a diamond, without losing a trick to the ♠ 10.

Unhesitatingly Jan Wohlin led the ♠ Q.

Always an honoured guest in my column is Britain's Sorcerer-in-Chief, Hugh Darwen, successor in *Bridge Magazine* to Commander Ernest Pawle, the most famous problemist of all time.

This piece of witchcraft was composed especially for me.

The bidding is immaterial and all four hands are assumed to be on view. The reader may like to take South's place before looking at the solution.

West leads the ♣ K against 3 NT. How should South play?

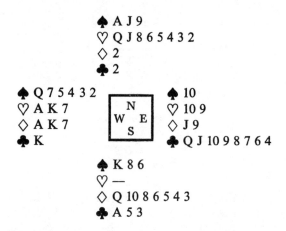

South wins and leads a spade. There are two variants.

1. West plays low. The trick is won by the ♠ J and the ♡ Q is led to West's ♡ K. The ♠ Q comes back. What next?
   South goes up with the ♠ A, carefully throwing under it his ♠ K. The ♡ J drives out the ♡ A and dummy's ♠ 9 is an entry to six good hearts.

2. West goes up at trick two with the ♠ Q. Now South adopts a different plan. Winning with the ♠ A, he leads a diamond, finessing against East. West's best return is a spade. Winning in his hand, South leads another diamond and throws on it dummy's ♠ J. West can only cash his tops, dummy's hearts and declarer's diamonds all being good.

The 30th April is Walpurgis night. The witches are out in force after dark riding on broomsticks to sup with their master, the Devil. The occasion calls for a spell by the sorcerer.

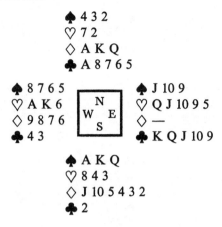

♠ 4 3 2
♡ 7 2
◇ A K Q
♣ A 8 7 6 5

♠ 8 7 6 5   ♠ J 10 9
♡ A K 6   ♡ Q J 10 9 5
◇ 9 8 7 6   ◇ —
♣ 4 3   ♣ K Q J 10 9

♠ A K Q
♡ 8 4 3
◇ J 10 5 4 3 2
♣ 2

CONTRACT 5 ◇ : LEAD ◇ 9

With ten top tricks declarer could make one more by ruffing a heart in dummy. Alas, having opened a trump, West is one move ahead, for of course he will lead trumps whenever he gets the chance. What's to be done?

Dummy's ♡ 7 holds the key. If West had it, instead of the ♡ 6, there would be no story to tell. As things are, declarer comes to hand with the ♠ A and leads the ♡ 3. West must win since East couldn't return a trump. A second trump from West is followed by the ♡ 7. Dummy's last trump goes, but so does West's second high heart and he is now out of the picture.

The spotlight turns on East. Declarer cashes his winners, leaving himself with the ♡ 8 and ♣ 2. Dummy's last two cards are the ♣ A 8. East squirms—and surrenders.

Here's another incantation by Hugh Darwen.

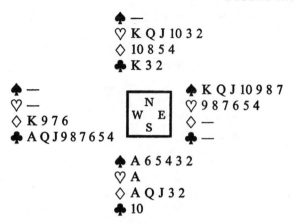

```
                    ♠ —
                    ♡ K Q J 10 3 2
                    ◊ 10 8 5 4
                    ♣ K 3 2
♠ —                                    ♠ K Q J 10 9 8 7
♡ —               ┌─────────┐          ♡ 9 8 7 6 5 4
◊ K 9 7 6         │    N    │          ◊ —
♣ A Q J 9 8 7 6 5 4│ W   E  │          ♣ —
                   │    S    │
                   └─────────┘
                    ♠ A 6 5 4 3 2
                    ♡ A
                    ◊ A Q J 3 2
                    ♣ 10
```

West leads the ♣ A, then the ♣ Q against 5 ◊. South can throw his ♡ A on the ♣ K, unblocking, and later pick up four hearts, but that still leaves him a trick short. What's to be done?

If, after an hour or so, the solution eludes the reader, here it is.

South ruffs the ♣ 3 high at trick two and leads the ◊ Q. West ducks, but must win the next diamond. A club to dummy's ♣ K follows. Unblocking in hearts won't help, while not to unblock would mean giving up hearts altogether. So now comes the key play. Declarer ruffs the ♣ K with the ◊ A! Next he leads the ◊ 2, finesses and cashes the ◊ 10.

East is down to six cards.

Unless he has kept two spades, all South's spades are good and if he has only four hearts, the ♡ A is jettisoned, at last, on the ◊ 10 and dummy has six winning hearts.

Walpurgis night comes round again, but our sorcerer isn't around to bewitch the cards. If you want a hand for the occasion —to slip in unobtrusively in a friendly duplicate, perhaps—try this one.

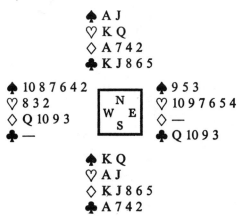

♠ A J
♡ K Q
◇ A 7 4 2
♣ K J 8 6 5

♠ 10 8 7 6 4 2   ♠ 9 5 3
♡ 8 3 2   ♡ 10 9 7 6 5 4
◇ Q 10 9 3   ◇ —
♣ —   ♣ Q 10 9 3

♠ K Q
♡ A J
◇ K J 8 6 5
♣ A 7 4 2

It is virtually impossible for North-South to keep out of a slam. With thirty-six points between them, they have more than enough.

Both 6 ♣ and 6 ◇ are eminently reasonable contracts and with match-points scoring many a pair will end up in 6 NT. Alas, even game can't be made. The witches will see to that.

Played in a minor, declarer will lose two trump tricks and one more in the other minor—two if he isn't careful.

In no trumps, South can only come to eight tricks. A lead in either major will drive out his first stopper, and when the defence gains the lead—in whichever minor declarer tries to set up—the second stopper will go. Thereafter, there will be no time to set up anything.

The other side of the medal is the famous Duke of Cumberland hand on which a grand slam is made on a mere six points.

No treatise on witchcraft would be complete without a final chapter by Giorgio Belladonna, the greatest magician of them all. Watch the cards do his bidding on a hand which came up in one of the qualifying rounds of the World Championship in Bermuda.

♠ 9 4 2
♡ K Q
♢ A K 8 3
♣ A 9 8 6

♠ Q 10   ♠ K J 8 7 5 3
♡ J 10 7 4 3   N   ♡ —
♢ 9 4   W   E   ♢ Q 10 7 2
♣ K Q 3 2   S   ♣ J 7 4

♠ A 6
♡ A 9 8 6 5 2
♢ J 6 5
♣ 10 5

CONTRACT 4 ♡: LEAD ♣ K

What is the predestined result?

Declarer has two trump losers and one in each of the other three suits. The prognosis is, therefore, two down.

But what happens if the physician in charge is Giorgio Belladonna? Quite right. He will cheat death and the patient will survive.

This was the treatment.

Going up with the ♣ A, Giorgio cashed the ♡ K and discovered the 5–0 break. A club, at trick two, was taken by East's ♣ J, and a spade came back.

Belladonna won, crossed to the ♡ Q and led a third club, discarding his losing spade.

Coming in with the ♣ Q, West returned the ♠ Q. Giorgio ruffed, cashed the ♢ A K and discarded his third diamond on the ♣ 6, while West followed suit helplessly.

In the three-card ending, with the lead in dummy, West sat with ♡ J 10 7 poised over declarer's ♡ A 9 8. Giorgio Belladonna ruffed dummy's last diamond with the ♡ 8, and West was well and truly end-played in trumps. Five losers had been telescoped into three.

More than a dozen important books on bridge are published every year. As a service to his readers, the bridge columnist should mention them, for if he doesn't, no one else will. In return, the books will provide him with rewarding material, and above all, with ideas.

Since magic has been our theme, I will start with *Bridge Magic*, published in 1973.

With the exception of a modest paperback published in America some years ago, no one, since the days of whist, has made a serious attempt to produce a book of double-dummy problems.

Hugh Darwen takes up the challenge and presents a fascinating collection of the world's greatest teasers.

Here is a single-dummy classic by Paul Lukacs.

♠ J 10 9 6 4
♡ 10 9 6 4 2
♢ Q 6 4
♣ —

♠ A Q
♡ A K J
♢ A K J 10
♣ A K J 10

CONTRACT 6 NT: LEAD ♢ 9

How can South make sure of twelve tricks against the best defence and the worst distribution?

If he lays down the ♠ A and continues with the ♠ Q, he is allowed to hold the trick. Now, when he loses the lead in hearts—and he cannot make twelve tricks without them—defenders will score the setting trick with the ♠ K.

The solution is to lead the ♠ Q at trick two. If defenders win, declarer has twelve tricks. If they don't, he leads the ♡ J. Again defenders must duck. Having retained control of both majors, South clears the clubs.

Le Dentu's *Bridge à la Une*, translated by Alan Truscott and Amalya Kearse, is now available in English under the title *Championship Bridge*. It was the first book I reviewed when I joined the *Evening Standard*. This was the hand I picked.

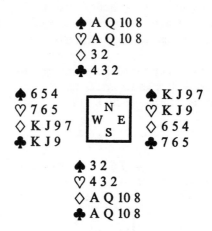

```
                    ♠ A Q 10 8
                    ♡ A Q 10 8
                    ◇ 3 2
                    ♣ 4 3 2

   ♠ 6 5 4          ┌─────┐        ♠ K J 9 7
   ♡ 7 6 5          │  N  │        ♡ K J 9
   ◇ K J 9 7        │W   E│        ◇ 6 5 4
   ♣ K J 9          │  S  │        ♣ 7 6 5
                    └─────┘
                    ♠ 3 2
                    ♡ 4 3 2
                    ◇ A Q 10 8
                    ♣ A Q 10 8
```

Playing in 3 NT, doubled, South could do no better than score his four aces and North, a notorious result-merchant, had many bitter things to say. Was the contract so very bad? That was the question put by an injured reader. Rallying to his defence, Le Dentu replied: 'Take your revenge.' Prepare the same deal and bet the result-merchant that you will make a grand slam in *any denomination*. I advise a small precaution. Interchange the East-West hands.

With every card right, just as every card was wrong before, South now makes not only 7 NT or 7 ♡, but even 7 ♠. After playing trumps twice through West—who now holds ♠ K J 9 7— declarer cashes three tricks in each of the other three suits, finessing as required, and leads a club or diamond at the twelfth trick. West is left with two spades and dummy sits over him with two better ones.

France, land of the bibliophile, as of the connoisseur in so many fields, has given birth to the most luxurious, the most ambitious and surely the most expensive of the many thousands of books on bridge.

Lavishly produced, *L'Aristocratie du Bridge,* by Alan Truscott, Pierre Jaïs and José Le Dentu, traces the history of the game, step by step, from Culbertson and the Bennett murder case to the Omar Sharif Circus and the come-back of Italy's Blue Team. Every theme is copiously illustrated with pictures of great personalities and great events.

Spectacular hands abound, like this one.

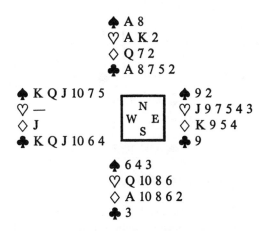

```
              ♠ A 8
              ♡ A K 2
              ◇ Q 7 2
              ♣ A 8 7 5 2
♠ K Q J 10 7 5   ┌─────┐   ♠ 9 2
♡ —              │  N  │   ♡ J 9 7 5 4 3
◇ J            W │     │ E ◇ K 9 5 4
♣ K Q J 10 6 4   │  S  │   ♣ 9
                 └─────┘
              ♠ 6 4 3
              ♡ Q 10 8 6
              ◇ A 10 8 6 2
              ♣ 3
```

How would you rate South's chances in 7 ♡? Impossible? On the contrary, unbeatable on any lead!

Let's say that West opens the ♠ K. Declarer wins and leads the ◇ Q, pinning West's ◇ J. Crossing to the ♣ A, he plays the ◇ 7, finessing. Dummy's ♠ 8 is discarded on South's fourth diamond and the last seven tricks are made on a cross-ruff, East under-ruffing six times!

Psychology, cheating, ethics, professionalism, everything comes under the spotlight. Each one of the authors has his contribution to make, but *primus inter pares,* I suspect, is José Le Dentu, a great player and a still greater writer.

Le Dentu's vivid pen sketches of France's leading players have often helped me to enliven my column. In *Bridge Facile,* still to be translated, I found the hand I needed to introduce Paul Chemla, when he was chosen to represent France in his first international at Athens in 1971.

The 'enfant terrible' of French bridge, as Le Dentu calls him, sat South here against the Blue Team's Pabis-Ticci and D'Alelio at a tournament in Morocco.

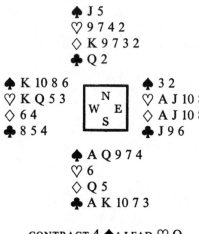

♠ J 5
♡ 9 7 4 2
◇ K 9 7 3 2
♣ Q 2

♠ K 10 8 6   ♠ 3 2
♡ K Q 5 3   ♡ A J 10 8
◇ 6 4   ◇ A J 10 8
♣ 8 5 4   ♣ J 9 6

♠ A Q 9 7 4
♡ 6
◇ Q 5
♣ A K 10 7 3

CONTRACT 4 ♠ : LEAD ♡ Q

After the ♡ Q—the Italians lead the second honour—came another heart and the kibitzers, seeing all four hands, began to wonder how badly Chemla would go down.

Ruffing the second heart, Paul Chemla led the ◇ Q to East's ◇ A, ruffed the heart continuation and crossing to the ◇ K, ruffed dummy's last heart. Next came the three top clubs, bringing declarer's total to seven tricks, and then a fourth club. With trumps only left, West was obliged to ruff. Chemla over-ruffed in dummy and continued with a diamond on which he threw a club. Still burdened with a trump too many, West had to ruff his partner's trick and to lead into the ♠ A Q.

Where was bridge born? The origin is obscure, but the word was used by the British colony in Constantinople before the turn of the century. Nascent bridge was akin to whist. The dealer named the trumps or passed the choice to his partner. Opponents could double, but otherwise stayed silent.

Honours were highly prized and spades had the lowest rank, hearts the highest.

One of the earliest books on bridge was *Pons Asinorum* published in 1899. Few copies exist today. Mine comes from Bibliagora, a venture by David Rex-Taylor, who sells only bridge literature, specializing in rare books of antiquarian interest.

Here's a hand from an expert game in Constantinople.

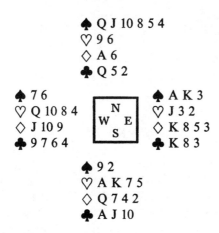

♠ Q J 10 8 5 4
♡ 9 6
◇ A 6
♣ Q 5 2

♠ 7 6
♡ Q 10 8 4
◇ J 10 9
♣ 9 7 6 4

♠ A K 3
♡ J 3 2
◇ K 8 5 3
♣ K 8 3

♠ 9 2
♡ A K 7 5
◇ Q 7 4 2
♣ A J 10

South deals and chooses to play in no trumps. He wins the heart lead and turns to spades. Winning with ♠ A, East boldly leads the ◇ K to knock out dummy's only entry. This is now called the *Merrimac Coup* and East was surely a fine natural player to find it at the table.

Instead of making game—there was no need to call it—South was kept to six tricks.

One of the unfulfilled ambitions of David Rex-Taylor—founder of the Richmond Congress, later to become the *Evening Standard* Charity Congress—is to win his own trophy, the Rex-Taylor Cup for Mixed Teams of Four. He looked like doing it once when, on the last set of boards, his hopes were dashed by world champion, Adam Meredith.

Meredith always had a penchant for psyching, more especially in spades. Third in hand, at favourable vulnerability, he couldn't resist the temptation here:

Dealer North: E/W Vul.

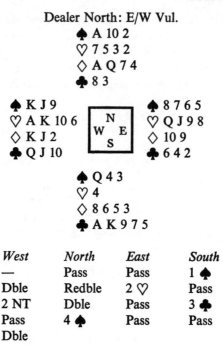

	♠ A 10 2	
	♡ 7 5 3 2	
	♦ A Q 7 4	
	♣ 8 3	

♠ K J 9		♠ 8 7 6 5
♡ A K 10 6		♡ Q J 9 8
♦ K J 2		♦ 10 9
♣ Q J 10		♣ 6 4 2

	♠ Q 4 3	
	♡ 4	
	♦ 8 6 5 3	
	♣ A K 9 7 5	

West	*North*	*East*	*South*
—	Pass	Pass	1 ♠
Dble	Redble	2 ♡	Pass
2 NT	Dble	Pass	3 ♣
Pass	4 ♠	Pass	Pass
Dble			

North should have suspected something, for there are only forty points in the pack. His 4 ♠ bid was unwise, to say the least, but it had a curious sequel.

West led the ♡ A K. Meredith ruffed, took the diamond finesse and ruffed another heart. Then he cashed the ♦ A and the ♣ A K, ruffed a club on the table and dummy's last heart with his ♠ Q. Another club, towards dummy's ♠ A 10, ensured two more tricks.

'The only game contract,' observed Meredith. Rex-Taylor was East.

Psychics make good material for the columnist. Used skilfully, they can, at times, put off the most experienced players. The example below is from the America-Lebanon match in the New York Olympiad in 1964. North-South were Dorothy Hayden and B. Jay Becker, one of America's great partnerships of the day.

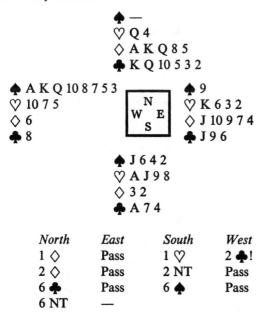

```
                        ♠ —
                        ♡ Q 4
                        ◇ A K Q 8 5
                        ♣ K Q 10 5 3 2
  ♠ A K Q 10 8 7 5 3                      ♠ 9
  ♡ 10 7 5              ┌─────────┐       ♡ K 6 3 2
  ◇ 6                   │   N     │       ◇ J 10 9 7 4
  ♣ 8                   │ W   E   │       ♣ J 9 6
                        │   S     │
                        └─────────┘
                        ♠ J 6 4 2
                        ♡ A J 9 8
                        ◇ 3 2
                        ♣ A 7 4
```

North	East	South	West
1 ◇	Pass	1 ♡	2 ♣ !
2 ◇	Pass	2 NT	Pass
6 ♣	Pass	6 ♠	Pass
6 NT	—		

The scales didn't fall from the eyes of B. Jay Becker, North, until Dorothy Hayden, South, bid 2 NT, showing that she, too, had clubs. It was clear to him then that West's 2 ♣ was pure bluff and too late he tried to expose it by leaping to 6 ♣. To Dorothy Hayden the bid conveyed quite a different message. Taking it as an esoteric demand for preference at the six level between diamonds and spades, she made the 'obvious' bid.

West passed gratefully and no less gratefully when Becker converted 6 ♠ to 6 NT. Then he proceeded to collect the first eight tricks. But for the confusion and misunderstandings caused by West's mischievous psychic, B. Jay Becker and Dorothy Hayden would have doubtless bid and made 6 ♣.

For one of the most spectacular psyches of all time we must go back to the France-Holland match of 1948. Sitting South is the intrepid Bob Slavenburg, playing in his first international.

Dealer East: E/W Vul.

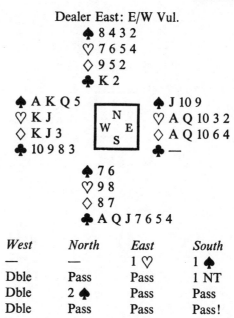

```
                    ♠ 8 4 3 2
                    ♡ 7 6 5 4
                    ◇ 9 5 2
                    ♣ K 2
    ♠ A K Q 5                      ♠ J 10 9
    ♡ K J            N             ♡ A Q 10 3 2
    ◇ K J 3       W     E          ◇ A Q 10 6 4
    ♣ 10 9 8 3       S            ♣ —
                    ♠ 7 6
                    ♡ 9 8
                    ◇ 8 7
                    ♣ A Q J 7 6 5 4
```

West	North	East	South
—	—	1 ♡	1 ♠
Dble	Pass	Pass	1 NT
Dble	2 ♠	Pass	Pass
Dble	Pass	Pass	Pass!

Of course, when Slavenburg started psyching, he intended to escape, eventually, into clubs. But North, an obstinate man, looked capable of going back to spades for a long, long time, so Bob decided to take his medicine.

To reduce ruffing value, West started with the ♠ A K Q, dropping East's ♠ J 10 9. A shock, but West had steady nerves. Since a switch to a red suit involved a guess, he led a club, just to be safe. Slavenburg promptly went up with dummy's ♣ K, drew the last trump and gathered six more clubs for his contract.

East-West, of course, can make a grand slam in three suits—including spades!

The next example is from a pairs event in Paris, where the competitors had the unusual experience of being informed every four boards exactly how they should have bid and played, for the same hands were presented simultaneously to four internationals at an 'exhibition table'.

Here European champions, Leon Tintner and Claude Deruy opposed Omar Sharif and Leon Yallouze.

Dealer South: E/W Vul.

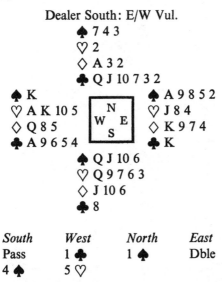

```
              ♠ 7 4 3
              ♡ 2
              ◇ A 3 2
              ♣ Q J 10 7 3 2
   ♠ K                          ♠ A 9 8 5 2
   ♡ A K 10 5      N            ♡ J 8 4
   ◇ Q 8 5      W     E         ◇ K 9 7 4
   ♣ A 9 6 5 4     S            ♣ K
              ♠ Q J 10 6
              ♡ Q 9 7 6 3
              ◇ J 10 6
              ♣ 8
```

South	West	North	East
Pass	1 ♣	1 ♠	Dble
4 ♠	5 ♡		

This bidding sequence isn't, strictly speaking, classical, not even at an exhibition table. Over Deruy's 1 ♣, Omar Sharif, North, decided to enliven proceedings with a psychic 1 ♠ and when Tintner doubled, Deruy hastened to explain that it was not a penalty, but a negative or Sputnik double, showing scattered values. Thereupon Yallouze bid a gallant 4 ♠, which must have thrilled Omar.

Refusing to be crowded out, Deruy sailed into 5 ♡. South passed happily.

'On your system,' asked Deruy, 'is it permitted to over-call on four-card suits?'

'Yes,' replied Yallouze, 'so long as they are good suits.'

The counterpart to a psychic bid is a psychic play. In his *Cent Donnes Extraordinaires*, José Le Dentu describes a brilliant piece of deception by Sophocles Venizelos, who once represented France at bridge and later became Prime Minister of Greece.

Dealer North: Love All

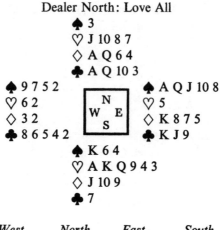

♠ 3
♡ J 10 8 7
◇ A Q 6 4
♣ A Q 10 3

♠ 9 7 5 2
♡ 6 2
◇ 3 2
♣ 8 6 5 4 2

♠ A Q J 10 8
♡ 5
◇ K 8 7 5
♣ K J 9

♠ K 6 4
♡ A K Q 9 4 3
◇ J 10 9
♣ 7

West	North	East	South
—	1 ◇	1 ♠	3 ♡
Pass	4 ♡	Pass	4 NT
Pass	5 ♡	Pass	6 ♡
Pass	Pass	Dble	

East won the first trick with the ♠ A and led a heart. The
contract is clearly unmakeable, but that didn't stop Venizelos
from making it. Expecting the diamond finesse to be wrong, he
calmly laid down the ◇ A and led the ◇ 4, as if he hoped to
bring down the ◇ K after two ruffs. East played low and Venizelos
won with the ◇ J. After ruffing a spade, Venizelos played off his
winners, leaving himself with the ◇ 10 and the ♣ 7. Dummy's
last two cards were the ♣ A Q and poor East, once so confident,
had to throw his ◇ K or bare his ♣ K.

Psychology can be a powerful aid to technique.

South deals. You sit West.

♠ J 5 4 3
♡ Q J 10 9 8
◇ 10 7
♣ K 6

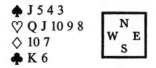

and you hear this bidding:

South	North
1 ♠	2 ♣
3 ♠	4 ♠
4 NT	5 ◇
5 NT	6 ◇
6 ♠	—

What should you lead? West, in a top-class game, was the American international, Lee Hazan, noted for his subtlety. This is how he reasoned: North's response to Blackwood showed an ace, presumably the ♣ A. If South needed the club finesse, he would take it anyway. But not knowing of the bad trump break, he might well think that he could afford to lose a club and he would be naturally reluctant to finesse at trick one, in case of a ruff.

Having read the message implicit in the bidding and peered into declarer's mind, Lee Hazan boldly underled his ♣ K. This was the deal.

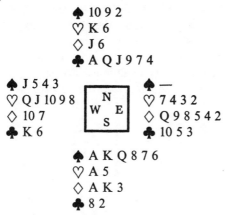

```
                  ♠ 10 9 2
                  ♡ K 6
                  ◇ J 6
                  ♣ A Q J 9 7 4

   ♠ J 5 4 3                    ♠ —
   ♡ Q J 10 9 8    N            ♡ 7 4 3 2
   ◇ 10 7       W     E         ◇ Q 9 8 5 4 2
   ♣ K 6           S            ♣ 10 5 3

                  ♠ A K Q 8 7 6
                  ♡ A 5
                  ◇ A K 3
                  ♣ 8 2
```

Of course, South went up with the ♣ A and lost this unbeatable slam. It is hard to blame him.

A feature of the next hand is that it was dealt to four comparatively inexperienced players. East was still at school.

Dealer South: N/S Vul.

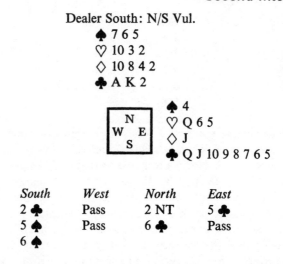

South	West	North	East
2 ♣	Pass	2 NT	5 ♣
5 ♠	Pass	6 ♣	Pass
6 ♠			

West opened the ♠ 2 to South's ♠ A. After two more rounds of trumps, West following, declarer led the ♡ J. West played the ♡ 7 and East, after a pause, the ♡ 5. An expert would have played low too, but not, perhaps, for the same reason.

The expert would guess that declarer had no club and was trying to create an entry in dummy. So playing low to the ♡ J would cost one trick and gain two. These were the other hands.

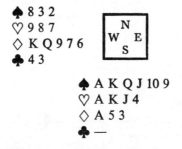

East admitted that he hadn't worked it out. 'South must have wanted me to take that ♡ J,' he explained, 'and if it was good for him, it was bad for me. So I didn't. I knew that I could trust him.'

That is the genesis of psychology. Just as technique often consists in reading the cards, so psychology lies in reading an opponent's mind.

For a sophisticated example let's go back to Lee Hazan, a master of applied psychology.

During the final stages of a big American tournament, Lee Hazan found himself in a critical contract which depended on losing no trick to the king of trumps. Three cards in the suit were out against him, so the percentage tables clearly indicated a finesse.

Lee Hazan led a trump from dummy up to his A Q, and as the next player followed low he paused to sense the atmosphere. Had he overlooked anything which could give a clue? While he was thinking, the player on his left hailed a passing waiter to order a coca-cola.

Describing the incident in *Collier's Magazine*, Lee Hazan writes: 'There and then I knew he had the missing king. No man orders a drink in the middle of a crucial hand unless he is trying to be too nonchalant. I played my ace and the king dropped.'

I have christened this hand *The Coca-Cola Coup*.

How do various coups get their names? The *Vienna Coup* doubtless originated in Vienna. Deschappelles was a great whist player, Merrimac a ship, while the *Devil's Coup* is just devilish. The *Morton Coup*, according to the American *Bridge World*, is named after Henry VII's Chancellor, who squeezed the nobles on this principle: if they lived well, they must be rich. If they lived simply, they obviously saved a lot. Either way, they had money for the king.

Here's an example of the *Morton Coup*.

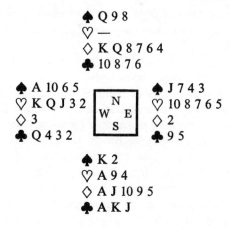

```
                    ♠ Q 9 8
                    ♡ —
                    ◇ K Q 8 7 6 4
                    ♣ 10 8 7 6
♠ A 10 6 5                          ♠ J 7 4 3
♡ K Q J 3 2      N                  ♡ 10 8 7 6 5
◇ 3            W   E                ◇ 2
♣ Q 4 3 2        S                  ♣ 9 5
                    ♠ K 2
                    ♡ A 9 4
                    ◇ A J 10 9 5
                    ♣ A K J
```

CONTRACT 6 ◇ : LEAD ♡ K

So long as West has the ♠ A, South can get his slam. Having no profitable discard to make on the ♡ A, declarer ruffs the ♡ K, crosses to his hand with a trump and leads the ♠ 2.

If West goes up with the ♠ A, the ♠ Q will yield South his twelfth trick. So West plays low, allowing the ♠ Q to win. South comes back with a trump, cashes the ♡ A, discarding a spade from dummy, and ruffs his last heart.

Now the ♠ K throws in West, who is forced to lead a club or to concede a ruff and discard.

A writer enjoys the privilege of conjuring up spirits to convey his messages. I have put three into orbit and may yet summon others.

Here's the Professor, so preoccupied with his bad luck that he has no time to guard against it. I see a lot of him, so he is entitled to several mentions.

Dealer South: Love All

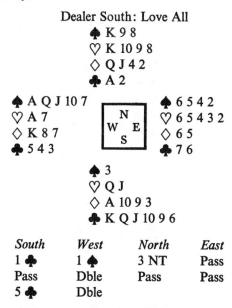

♠ K 9 8
♡ K 10 9 8
◇ Q J 4 2
♣ A 2

♠ A Q J 10 7
♡ A 7
◇ K 8 7
♣ 5 4 3

♠ 6 5 4 2
♡ 6 5 4 3 2
◇ 6 5
♣ 7 6

♠ 3
♡ Q J
◇ A 10 9 3
♣ K Q J 10 9 6

South	West	North	East
1 ♣	1 ♠	3 NT	Pass
Pass	Dble	Pass	Pass
5 ♣	Dble		

West led the ♠ A, then the ♠ Q. The Professor, who was South, won with dummy's ♠ K and threw a diamond from his hand. On the bidding, East could hardly have the ◇ K, so at trick three the Professor led a heart, hoping to set up discards for his two remaining diamonds. West, however, went up with the ♡ A and promptly returned another heart, and since he could ruff the next one, the suit was dead.

'At least we had honours,' remarked the Professor, 'and since West has three trumps, 5 ♣ is unmakeable.'

'Unbeatable,' retorted the Senior Kibitzer. 'You ruff the second spade, draw trumps and lead the ♡ Q. If West wins, you have three discards for your diamonds. If he ducks, you overtake, throw the ♡ J on your ♠ K and concede a diamond. A poor double of 3 NT,' added S.K. turning to West, 'the one contract you liked.'

'I had to make sure that despite the confident bidding, East would lead a spade,' explained West.

'I knew from the start', sighed East, 'that it would all be my fault.'

'There's nothing I dislike more than blind guesses,' said the Professor with feeling, as he inscribed 50 in the 'They' column.

Dealer East: Love All

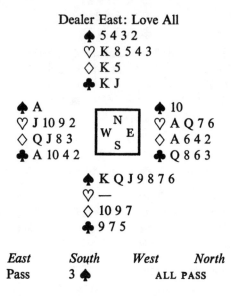

♠ 5 4 3 2
♡ K 8 5 4 3
◇ K 5
♣ K J

♠ A
♡ J 10 9 2
◇ Q J 8 3
♣ A 10 4 2

♠ 10
♡ A Q 7 6
◇ A 6 4 2
♣ Q 8 6 3

♠ K Q J 9 8 7 6
♡ —
◇ 10 9 7
♣ 9 7 5

East	South	West	North
Pass	3 ♠		ALL PASS

West led the ♡ J. The Professor played low from dummy, ruffed and led a trump to West's ace. West returned the ♣ 2 and the Professor went into a huddle. East clearly had the ♡ A and West had produced the ♠ A. Honours were even and either defender could have the ♣ A. After looking round vainly for inspiration, the Professor inserted the ♣ J, lost to East's ♣ Q and voiced his dislike for blind guesses.

'You should have gone up with the ♣ K,' the Senior Kibitzer told him sternly. 'East had passed, so how could he have the ♣ A as well as the ♡ A Q and the ◇ A?'

'Who said that he had the ◇ A?' protested the Professor.

'You should have done—softly to yourself,' replied S.K., 'for if West had the ◇ A, you couldn't lose anyway. So you should have placed East with it, in which case he couldn't have the ♣ A. Not such a blind guess after all, is it?'

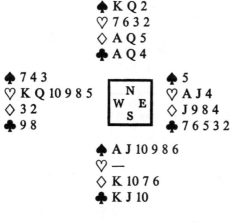

♠ K Q 2
♥ 7 6 3 2
♦ A Q 5
♣ A Q 4

♠ 7 4 3
♥ K Q 10 9 8 5
♦ 3 2
♣ 9 8

♠ 5
♥ A J 4
♦ J 9 8 4
♣ 7 6 5 3 2

♠ A J 10 9 8 6
♥ —
♦ K 10 7 6
♣ K J 10

CONTRACT 7 ♠: LEAD ♥ K

The Professor, sitting South, looked approvingly at dummy. Seeing no losers, he was about to table his hand when he realized that he didn't have thirteen winners either.

When the trumps split 3–1, the diamonds presented a problem. If they broke 3–3 against the odds, all would be well. If not, there was still a chance that the defender who was short in diamonds wouldn't have a third trump. Leaving the ♠ K in dummy, the Professor tried to take three rounds of diamonds. West ruffed and that was that.

'Just my luck,' cried the Professor bitterly. 'If the spades break or the diamonds break or if East has the long trump, the contract is cold. Why is everything always wrong?'

'The hearts weren't wrong,' observed the Senior Kibitzer.

'What have the hearts to do with it?' demanded the Professor indignantly.

'Had you ruffed out the hearts,' replied S.K., 'you would have seen East show out. That would have told you that West had six, as well as three spades. If he followed to two clubs, he couldn't have more than two diamonds, so, in all confidence you could have finessed against East.'

Dealer South: Love All

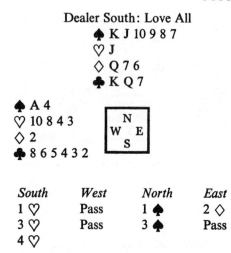

♠ K J 10 9 8 7
♡ J
◇ Q 7 6
♣ K Q 7

♠ A 4
♡ 10 8 4 3
◇ 2
♣ 8 6 5 4 3 2

South	West	North	East
1 ♡	Pass	1 ♠	2 ◇
3 ♡	Pass	3 ♠	Pass
4 ♡			

The Professor, sitting West, showed restraint by not doubling, but as the Senior Kibitzer was quick to point out, if he intended to defend as he did, he was right not to double.

The ◇ 2 lead was an immediate success. East won the first three tricks with the ◇ J, ◇ K and ◇ A, declarer following all the way. The Professor shed a spade and a club, and was sorry that he hadn't doubled. East led a fourth diamond. Declarer ruffed with the ♡ 2 and the Professor over-ruffed with the ♡ 3— not that it mattered, for by now the defence was helpless.

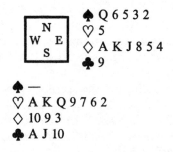

♠ Q 6 5 3 2
♡ 5
◇ A K J 8 5 4
♣ 9

♠ —
♡ A K Q 9 7 6 2
◇ 10 9 3
♣ A J 10

Dummy's ♡ J won the trick and it only remained for declarer to draw trumps.

The Professor was about to berate his partner when he saw South's hand. 'No spade at all? Ah well, you couldn't help it. The contract is unbreakable.'

'Unmakeable,' retorted the Senior Kibitzer. 'All you had to do was to throw your ♠ A. Partner would have surely noticed it, led a spade and you would have scored a trump trick.'

Here's another example from the Professor series. 'It isn't the good players, it's the good guessers who win the money,' lamented the Professor. The wrong guess had been expensive on this hand.

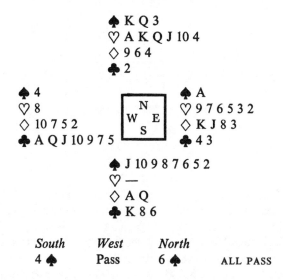

```
              ♠ K Q 3
              ♡ A K Q J 10 4
              ◇ 9 6 4
              ♣ 2

♠ 4                          ♠ A
♡ 8              N           ♡ 9 7 6 5 3 2
◇ 10 7 5 2   W     E         ◇ K J 8 3
♣ A Q J 10 9 7 5  S          ♣ 4 3

              ♠ J 10 9 8 7 6 5 2
              ♡ —
              ◇ A Q
              ♣ K 8 6
```

South	West	North	
4 ♠	Pass	6 ♠	ALL PASS

West led the ◇ 2. The Professor, East, played the ◇ K and the ◇ A won. Next came a trump. Winning with the ♠ A, the Professor had to take a critical decision. If declarer had a loser, was it a club or a diamond? 'A blind guess,' he declared, 'and with my luck I guessed wrong, of course.'

Even the Senior Kibitzer conceded that South was as likely to have the ◇ Q as the ♣ A and vice versa. 'And yet,' he said, 'you should have broken that contract, for though you couldn't tell about the ♣ A, you could have placed the ◇ Q.'

'How?' asked the Professor.

'By playing the ◇ J, not the ◇ K at trick one,' replied S.K.

'West wouldn't have underled an ace, but he might have played from a queen, so had the ♢ J been taken by the ♢ A, you would return a diamond. Seeing the ♢ Q win, you would play back a club.'

Who is the Senior Kibitzer? Has he flesh and bones or is he just another figment of the writer's imagination? S.K. is real and the next hand reveals his identity.

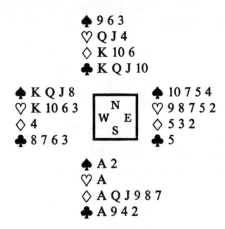

```
              ♠ 9 6 3
              ♡ Q J 4
              ♢ K 10 6
              ♣ K Q J 10

♠ K Q J 8                      ♠ 10 7 5 4
♡ K 10 6 3       N             ♡ 9 8 7 5 2
♢ 4           W     E          ♢ 5 3 2
♣ 8 7 6 3        S             ♣ 5

              ♠ A 2
              ♡ A
              ♢ A Q J 9 8 7
              ♣ A 9 4 2
```

This deal came up in the big game at the Eccentric Club, North-South finishing unhappily in 7 ♢. And yet 7 ♣, despite the 4–1 break, is unbeatable. Declarer cashes the ♡ A and ruffs a heart in the closed hand for his thirteenth trick.

It isn't hard to reach 7 ♣, if North responds 3 ♣ to South's opening 2 ♢. Most experts who were shown the hand preferred, however, an immediate raise to 3 ♢. Thereafter, each player in turn has trouble in convincing partner that he isn't cue-bidding, but has a real club suit.

A solution which appeals to me strongly was suggested by Stanley Merkin, doyen of the Kibitzers Corps at the Eccentric, as he was for so long at Crockfords. This is Merkin's sequence.

South	North
2 ♢	3 ♢
4 ♣	6 ♣ !

The unconventional jump raise of what sounds like a cue-bid must show, by inference, a suit with tops and no other feature of note. South counts up to thirteen and bids 7 ♣.

The Guardian Angel is at the top of his profession. He does his stuff nobly and his protégé always knows which card to play—though only a split second after he has played the wrong one.

'Please, Guardian Angel,' pleaded South, 'could I, just for a change, get a really lucky break, the sort my opponents always seem to get?' With a friendly nod, the G.A. struck a magic chord on her harp.

Dealer West: Love All

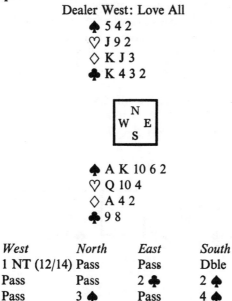

♠ 5 4 2
♡ J 9 2
◇ K J 3
♣ K 4 3 2

♠ A K 10 6 2
♡ Q 10 4
◇ A 4 2
♣ 9 8

West	North	East	South
1 NT (12/14)	Pass	Pass	Dble
Pass	Pass	2 ♣	2 ♠
Pass	3 ♠	Pass	4 ♠

West led the ♡ K, ♡ A and ♡ 3, and to South's relief, East followed. On the ♠ A K West dropped obligingly the ♠ Q J and when South led a club, dummy's ♣ K held. The G.A. wasn't letting him down. What was the right continuation?

As South led the ◇ A and ◇ 2, the G.A.'s wings twitched nervously. Confidently South inserted the ◇ J.

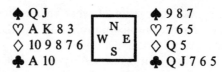

♠ Q J
♡ A K 8 3
◇ 10 9 8 7 6
♣ A 10

♠ 9 8 7
♡ 7 6 5
◇ Q 5
♣ Q J 7 6 5

There was a rasping noise on the harp as East's ◇ Q won and suddenly the scales fell from South's eyes. West had shown up already with fourteen points, a maximum for his 1 NT. He couldn't possibly have the ◇ Q as well. No G.A. could have done more than give him five diamonds, but the thoughtless South had failed to take advantage of his good fortune.

'I wish,' said South to his Guardian Angel on another occasion, 'that I could have one of those nice no trump hands that my opponents are always getting, two or three points to spare, every suit twice guarded and a friendly lead. The G.A. made a magic sign.

Dealer North: Game All

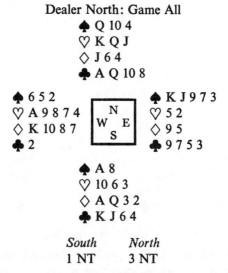

♠ Q 10 4
♡ K Q J
◇ J 6 4
♣ A Q 10 8

♠ 6 5 2
♡ A 9 8 7 4
◇ K 10 8 7
♣ 2

♠ K J 9 7 3
♡ 5 2
◇ 9 5
♣ 9 7 5 3

♠ A 8
♡ 10 6 3
◇ A Q 3 2
♣ K J 6 4

South	*North*
1 NT	3 NT

West led the ♡ 7. South looked at his watch and decided that, yes, he would have time for another rubber. Not bothering about overtricks, he began with the diamond finesse, losing to West's ◇ K. The spade return was covered by the ♠ 10, ♠ J and ♣ A, and when the diamonds broke 4–2, South discovered that he had to let West in again, to set up his ninth trick. West led another spade and it was all over.

The G.A. flapped a wing angrily and the scales fell from South's eyes.

At trick two, he should have crossed to the ♣ K and led a diamond towards dummy. If West played the ♢ K, he would have nine tricks. If the ♢ J held or if East had the ♢ K, there would be time to set up a second heart.

The Witch Doctor is declarer's best friend. As dummy goes down, the temperature drops and there's a sinister murmur 'abracadabra, abracadabra'. Knowing that the cards are bewitched, declarer looks for bad breaks and seeks ways to guard against them.

Dealer North: Love All

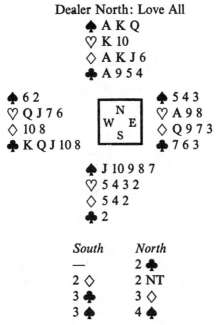

```
              ♠ A K Q
              ♡ K 10
              ♢ A K J 6
              ♣ A 9 5 4
  ♠ 6 2                        ♠ 5 4 3
  ♡ Q J 7 6      N             ♡ A 9 8
  ♢ 10 8       W   E           ♢ Q 9 7 3
  ♣ K Q J 10 8     S           ♣ 7 6 3
              ♠ J 10 9 8 7
              ♡ 5 4 3 2
              ♢ 5 4 2
              ♣ 2
```

South	North
—	2 ♣
2 ♢	2 NT
3 ♣	3 ♢
3 ♠	4 ♠

South might have passed 2 NT, but the temptation to look for a major suit fit, via Stayman, proved too strong.

West led the ♣ K and declarer could see eight tricks. The diamond finesse and 3–3 break would bring the total to ten, but that was too much to expect. A better chance was to find West with the ♡ A and to score the tenth trick by ruffing a heart in dummy.

Declarer was about to try it, when he saw the Witch Doctor hovering around. With him about, no finesse was likely to succeed, so South looked for something better.

At trick two, he ruffed a club. Crossing to dummy with the ◇ A and ◇ K he ruffed two more clubs. Then he exited with his third diamond and spread his hand, claiming ten tricks—dummy's ♠ A K Q, the ◇ A K, the ♣ A and four ruffs in the closed hand. He had ruffed three clubs and no one could stop him from ruffing dummy's fourth diamond.

Both in bidding and in the play, this was a bad hand for the Witch Doctor.

Dealer East: Game All

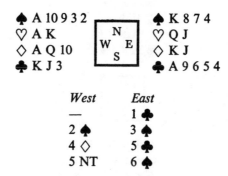

```
♠ A 10 9 3 2            ♠ K 8 7 4
♡ A K          N        ♡ Q J
◇ A Q 10    W   E       ◇ K J
♣ K J 3        S        ♣ A 9 6 5 4
```

West	East
—	1 ♣
2 ♠	3 ♠
4 ◇	5 ♣
5 NT	6 ♠

The Witch Doctor's incantation had ensured plenty of duplication and he had hopes that East-West would soar to 7 ♠. They were saved by Josephine, the 5 NT grand slam force, which called on East to bid 7 ♠ if he had two of the three top honours.

North opened a heart. To the second trick, West led the ♠ 2, North's card being the ♠ J. How should declarer continue?

The Witch Doctor had seen to it, of course, that the ♣ Q would be wrong, and so potent was his spell, that no matter how West played the trumps, he would lose one. If he went for the drop, North would show out. If he finessed, North would produce the ♠ Q. No Witch Doctor could do more, and yet West made his contract.

Winning with the ♠ K, he cashed dummy's ◊ K J, crossed to his hand with the ♡ A and continued with the ◊ A—ruffing in dummy! Next he led a trump, and as South followed, he spread his hand, announcing that he would take the finesse. If it succeeded, all would be well. If it failed, North would have to lead a club or to concede a ruff and discard. Either way, the spell was broken.

Being no ghost, and having none, I can afford to enjoy my foibles and fancies, to express my likes and dislikes, in short, to be my unhaunted self.

At Budget-time I like to give the Chancellor good advice, though he doesn't always follow it.

In 1971 I suggested a swingeing levy on fatuous signals. I still commend it as a tax that would benefit the payer even more than the Exchequer. Here's an example:

Dealer West: Love All

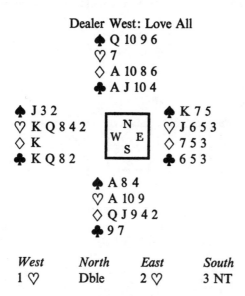

```
            ♠ Q 10 9 6
            ♡ 7
            ◊ A 10 8 6
            ♣ A J 10 4

♠ J 3 2              ♠ K 7 5
♡ K Q 8 4 2     N    ♡ J 6 5 3
◊ K          W     E ◊ 7 5 3
♣ K Q 8 2       S    ♣ 6 5 3

            ♠ A 8 4
            ♡ A 10 9
            ◊ Q J 9 4 2
            ♣ 9 7
```

West	North	East	South
1 ♡	Dble	2 ♡	3 NT

West opened the ♡ 4 to East's ♡ J. A heart to the ♡ Q came back, South playing low. Which heart should West play at trick three, the ♡ K, ♡ 8 or ♡ 2?

Among experts, real or imaginary, every pip tells a story

and when West chose the deuce, he showed an unmistakable interest in clubs, the lowest-ranking suit. Would he do that with one finessible honour? Never. So he clearly had both. East doubtless read the message, but so did South, who alone could profit by it.

As South ran the diamonds, he watched West squirm. He had to keep the ♣ K Q and two hearts, otherwise South could afford to lose the lead. So, in the five-card ending, West had room for one spade only. The ♠ K? Hardly, since he had signalled for a club.

Seizing his chance, South led dummy's ♠ Q, forcing East's ♠ K and scooping West's ♠ J.

Many will regret that there has never been a tax on conventions. It would have been a good vote catcher. Some signals, notably Suit Preference Signals (McKenney), lend themselves admirably to abuse. Here is an example from Crockfords, shortly before the club closed its doors.

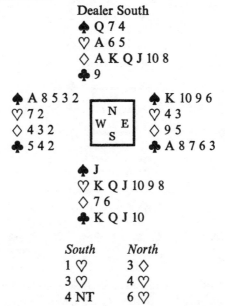

Dealer South

	♠ Q 7 4	
	♡ A 6 5	
	◇ A K Q J 10 8	
	♣ 9	

♠ A 8 5 3 2		♠ K 10 9 6
♡ 7 2	N	♡ 4 3
◇ 4 3 2	W E	◇ 9 5
♣ 5 4 2	S	♣ A 8 7 6 3

	♠ J	
	♡ K Q J 10 9 8	
	◇ 7 6	
	♣ K Q J 10	

South	*North*
1 ♡	3 ◇
3 ♡	4 ♡
4 NT	6 ♡

West led the ♠ A. Should East encourage? Reasoning that

with a void, South wouldn't have applied Blackwood, East decided rightly to call for a club switch. How could he do it? The ♠ 10 or ♠ 9 would ask for another spade, while the ♠ 6 would be uninformative. East found the answer. On the ♠ A he threw the ♠ K! With the ♠ Q in dummy, the demand for a switch was clear. West got the message, but read it, alas, as a suit preference signal, an 'unnecessarily' high card and therefore a request for diamonds, the higher-ranking suit.

Wouldn't East have played the ♠ K had he wanted to ruff diamonds? Yet another convention gives the answer. With a void, East would have doubled, the Lightner lead-directing slam double. That one, fortunately, is rarely abused and could stay untaxed.

I have never taken kindly to the plethora of gadgets and conventions which disfigure competitive bridge and keep so many players away from duplicate. Admittedly, happy-go-lucky methods wouldn't ensure success at the summit, though even at the summit there's no need to replace every natural bid by two that are artificial. As for the weekly pairs at the local club, I am certain that most competitors would play better and enjoy the game far more if a dip into the refreshing waters of Lethe made them forget all that they had ever learnt about codes and cyphers and pseudo-scientific methods.

It's an awesome thought that Amalya Kearse's *Bridge Conventions Complete* runs to 624 pages!

I confess that the discomfiture of the eggheads gives me pleasure. All my examples of the chaos and confusion to which their acrobatics so often lead are culled from records of events on the highest plane.

That ubiquitous but indefinable being, 'the average player', may find it reassuring to peer at the giants' feet of clay—and amusing, too, I hope, to see them slip on their own banana skins.

Our first example comes from the Official Handbook on the 1972 Olympiad.

For the first time, the same computer-dealt hands were played in all the matches, allowing results to be compared over the whole field.

This one was unique:

Dealer South: N/S Vul.

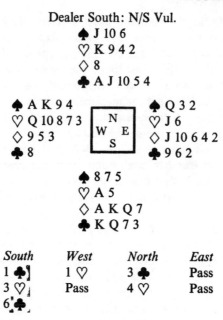

♠ J 10 6
♡ K 9 4 2
◇ 8
♣ A J 10 5 4

♠ A K 9 4   ♠ Q 3 2
♡ Q 10 8 7 3   ♡ J 6
◇ 9 5 3   ◇ J 10 6 4 2
♣ 8   ♣ 9 6 2

♠ 8 7 5
♡ A 5
◇ A K Q 7
♣ K Q 7 3

South	West	North	East
1 ♣	1 ♡	3 ♣	Pass
3 ♡	Pass	4 ♡	Pass
6 ♣			

Sitting East-West for France against China were Gérard Bourtchtoff and Claude Delmouly, winners of the first Bridge Olympiad. Against a lesser pair the slam would have stood no chance, but this is what happened.

Bourtchtoff led the ♠ K and Delmouly dropped the ♠ 2. This was not a denial, but a count signal, showing an odd number of spades. Could it be three? Surely not, for what declarer would bid a slam with three quick losers?

Concluding that partner had five spades and declarer a singleton, Bourtchtoff switched to a heart. Maybe Delmouly would ruff it.

Declarer promptly discarded dummy's two spades on his diamonds and cross-ruffed the rest.

Still at the Olympiad, the two scientists had another opportunity to put their advanced theories into practice. The occasion was the match between France and Italy.

Dealer West: N/S Vul.

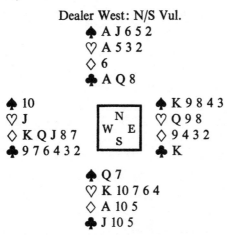

♠ A J 6 5 2
♥ A 5 3 2
♦ 6
♣ A Q 8

♠ 10
♥ J
♦ K Q J 8 7
♣ 9 7 6 4 3 2

♠ K 9 8 4 3
♥ Q 9 8
♦ 9 4 3 2
♣ K

♠ Q 7
♥ K 10 7 6 4
♦ A 10 5
♣ J 10 5

Both North-Souths reached 6 ♥. With the cards badly placed, the French declarer, Klotz, went down. Sitting East-West in the other room were Bourtchtoff and Delmouly and here events took a very different turn.

During the auction, the French, looking for a sacrifice, bid diamonds, and when South called 6 ♥, Delmouly, West, doubled. This, in accordance with a sophisticated convention, meant, not that he hoped to defeat the slam, but the exact opposite—that he hadn't a single defensive trick.

With such valuable information at his command, declarer could hardly go wrong. He would take the right view in trumps and maybe even drop the singleton ♣ K.

Seeing his considerable defensive values shrink to nothing, Bourtchtoff sacrificed in 7 ♦. A cheap save—after an expensive double.

The French have no monopoly of science. An American pair, who shall be nameless, are the stars on the next deal which came up in a qualifying round during the World Championship of 1975 in Bermuda.

Dealer North: N/S Vul.

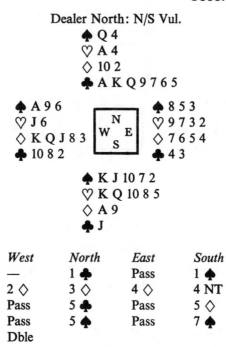

```
                      ♠ Q 4
                      ♡ A 4
                      ◇ 10 2
                      ♣ A K Q 9 7 6 5
  ♠ A 9 6                              ♠ 8 5 3
  ♡ J 6              ┌─────────┐       ♡ 9 7 3 2
  ◇ K Q J 8 3       │    N    │       ◇ 7 6 5 4
  ♣ 10 8 2          │  W   E  │       ♣ 4 3
                     │    S    │
                     └─────────┘
                      ♠ K J 10 7 2
                      ♡ K Q 10 8 5
                      ◇ A 9
                      ♣ J
```

West	North	East	South
—	1 ♣	Pass	1 ♠
2 ◇	3 ◇	4 ◇	4 NT
Pass	5 ♣	Pass	5 ◇
Pass	5 ♠	Pass	7 ♠
Dble			

What happened?

North thought that the agreed suit was clubs. His 5 ♣ response
to 4 NT was what is known as Key Card Blackwood—the king
of trumps being treated as an ace.

South believed that spades was the agreed suit and that North
was showing three aces. Yes, 5 ♣ promised three aces or none, all
very scientific.

The double of 7 ♠ sowed doubt in South's mind. The sight of
dummy quickly removed it. What would they say at the local
club if you ended up in a grand slam, missing the ace of trumps?

Nemesis finds it hard to catch up with every flight of conventional fancy and many an extravaganza escapes the punishment
it deserves, as on this hand in the Play Off to choose America's
team for the 1973 World Championship.

Dealer West: N/S Vul.

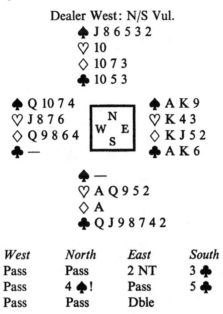

	North	East	South
West	*North*	*East*	*South*
Pass	Pass	2 NT	3 ♣
Pass	4 ♠!	Pass	5 ♣
Pass	Pass	Dble	

There was a gasp from the Vu-Graph audience when the Closed Room result was announced—5 ♣ doubled, made against East's 21 count. The play was simple. South won the diamond lead, cashed the ♡ A and ruffed two hearts, bringing down the ♡ K. The ♣ A K were his only losers.

What of North's remarkable jump to 4 ♠? He explained later that he took South's 3 ♣ to be conventional, showing support for both majors.

We cross the Atlantic for the European Championships in Ostend. This time, strange as was the bidding, the play was stranger still.

Dealer West: N/S Vul.

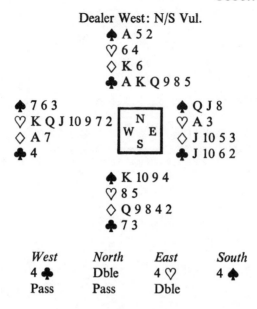

West	North	East	South
4 ♣	Dble	4 ♡	4 ♠
Pass	Pass	Dble	

West's 4 ♣ was South African Texas, a transfer bid designed to make East declarer in 4 ♡. Had West's hearts and spades been reversed, he would have bid 4 ◇ and East would have transferred to 4 ♠.

North's double showed presumably a club suit and all-round strength. South, however, seems to have interpreted it as a take-out double, though even so, he might have passed East's 4 ♡— especially if he intended to play as he did!

West led his ♣ 4. Winning with the ♣ A, declarer laid down the ♠ K, then the ♠ A, and continued with a second club. West ruffed joyfully and put East in with the ♡ A to play the ♠ Q. This left declarer with one trump to stem the avalanche of hearts, while West still retained the ◇ A.

The resulting penalty of 1,700 was easily a record up to that point in the European Championships.

We switch to rubber bridge. The standard is still high, but we are playing only for money, so we can relax and enjoy ourselves.

As at duplicate, the way to the worst contracts is often paved with the best conventions. The second best are usually less deadly. Not being so sophisticated, they are less readily mis-understood.

Roman Blackwood, more subtle than the original, is an ex-ample. We saw a variation of it recently when an American pair landed in a grand slam without the ace of trumps.

On Roman Blackwood a 5 ♣ response to 4 NT shows no ace *or three aces.* So wide is the gulf that no confusion can arise—in theory. This is what can happen in practice.

Dealer South: Love All

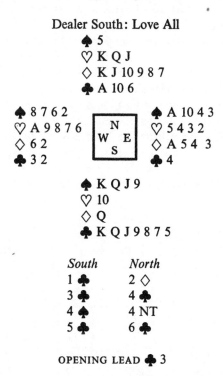

```
              ♠ 5
              ♡ K Q J
              ◇ K J 10 9 8 7
              ♣ A 10 6
  ♠ 8 7 6 2                ♠ A 10 4 3
  ♡ A 9 8 7 6      N       ♡ 5 4 3 2
  ◇ 6 2        W     E     ◇ A 5 4 3
  ♣ 3 2            S       ♣ 4
              ♠ K Q J 9
              ♡ 10
              ◇ Q
              ♣ K Q J 9 8 7 5
```

South	North
1 ♣	2 ◇
3 ♣	4 ♣
4 ♠	4 NT
5 ♣	6 ♣

OPENING LEAD ♣ 3

It hadn't dawned on North, of course, that South could be aceless. West proved to be equally unsuspecting.

South's expression gave nothing away as he studied dummy. Neither did he draw West's second trump. Had he done so, East would have signalled with the ♠ 10 and the cat would have been out of the bag. At trick two, declarer led a heart. Winning with the ♡ A, West innocently played a second trump and Roman Blackwood came into its own with a vengeance. Throwing the ◇ Q on the ♡ K, South set up the diamonds to take care of the of the spades. East's two aces 'also ran'.

Next to my 'Chaos and Conventions' file is one entitled 'Man Bites Dog'. The material sometimes overlaps, for though the emphasis is different, the theme is the same—the fallibility of the masters. They make mistakes, silly ones at that, and as in the case of lesser mortals, they may be due to temperament, thoughtlessness or the desire to be too clever.

The savant sequences we see in print are the work of established partnerships, players who have faced each other in countless tournaments and have discussed, again and again, the implications of every bid in every situation.

What happens when two champions play together for the first time—or only the tenth for that matter?

Here is an example from the France-Brazil match in the last qualifying round of the 1971 World Championship. With their place in the finals assured, the French were trying out a new formation, Roger Trézel opposite Jean-Louis Stoppa.

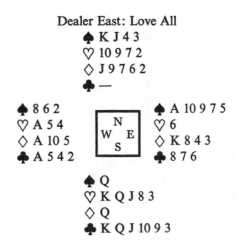

Dealer East: Love All

```
              ♠ K J 4 3
              ♡ 10 9 7 2
              ◇ J 9 7 6 2
              ♣ —
  ♠ 8 6 2            N        ♠ A 10 9 7 5
  ♡ A 5 4       W       E     ♡ 6
  ◇ A 10 5           S        ◇ K 8 4 3
  ♣ A 5 4 2                   ♣ 8 7 6
              ♠ Q
              ♡ K Q J 8 3
              ◇ Q
              ♣ K Q J 10 9 3
```

West	North	East	South
—	—	Pass	1 ♣
Pass	1 ◇	Pass	1 ♡
Pass	3 ♡	Pass	4 NT
Pass	5 ♣	Pass	7 ♡
Dble			

Trézel, South, expected a good deal more from North for his jump raise in hearts, so he applied Blackwood—the original version. Here, the 5 ♣ response has two alternative meanings— no aces or all four. Trézel reasoned that since an aceless hand didn't fit in with Stoppa's bidding, he must have all four.

'It might have been worse,' he observed philosophically after going three down. 'East could have had the ♣ A. Or I might have redoubled.'

Contrary to popular belief, the greatest players are human. It's comforting to think that Giorgio Belladonna, World Master Number One, has revoked twice at critical moments in international matches. And here's Pietro Forquet, then World Master Number Two, in the finals of the Olympiad in 1972.

Dealer West: E/W Vul.

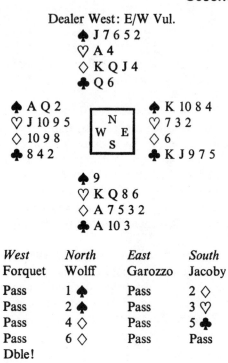

♠ J 7 6 5 2
♡ A 4
◇ K Q J 4
♣ Q 6

♠ A Q 2   ♠ K 10 8 4
♡ J 10 9 5   ♡ 7 3 2
◇ 10 9 8   ◇ 6
♣ 8 4 2   ♣ K J 9 7 5

♠ 9
♡ K Q 8 6
◇ A 7 5 3 2
♣ A 10 3

West	North	East	South
Forquet	Wolff	Garozzo	Jacoby
Pass	1 ♠	Pass	2 ◇
Pass	2 ♠	Pass	3 ♡
Pass	4 ◇	Pass	5 ♣
Pass	6 ◇	Pass	Pass
Dble!			

The slam is, perhaps, a trifle optimistic, but the curious feature of the bidding is not the contract, so much as Forquet's double. What does it mean?

Simple. Pietro thought that spades had been bid under him, not over him, and that it would be not his lead, but his partner's. So he doubled for a spade lead!

When the facts of life were revealed to him, Forquet led a club and beat the contract. The spade lead he wanted would have allowed declarer to make the slam by ruffing three spades in his hand and setting up the fifth spade in dummy.

The spotlight is still on Forquet, but two years have elapsed and the scene shifts from Miami to Venice. There are times when Pietro—like Oscar Wilde—can resist anything but temptation.

Dealer East: N/S Vul.

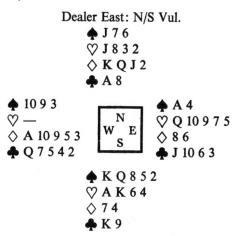

♠ J 7 6
♡ J 8 3 2
◇ K Q J 2
♣ A 8

♠ 10 9 3   ♠ A 4
♡ —   ♡ Q 10 9 7 5
◇ A 10 9 5 3   ◇ 8 6
♣ Q 7 5 4 2   ♣ J 10 6 3

♠ K Q 8 5 2
♡ A K 6 4
◇ 7 4
♣ K 9

In both rooms, South opened 1 ♠, rebid 2 ♡ on the next round, and was raised to 4 ♡ by North.

Sammy Kehela, once a teacher at the London School of Bridge, who sat East for North America, passed quietly and collected 200 as his just reward.

For the Italians, Pietro Forquet couldn't resist the temptation to double. Forewarned, North retreated promptly to 4 ♠ and Forquet doubled again—out of self-respect, no doubt—but there was no longer joy in his heart.

West opened the ◇ A and continued the suit. Rising with the ♠ A at trick three, Forquet led a heart. Declarer, Mark Blumenthal, played low and West ruffed, but the defence had no more tricks to make and the Americans duly chalked up 790—a swing of 990 or 14 IMPs.

The axiom: 'Never disturb opponents when you have them where you want them' again came into its own.

Elan, panache, bravura are not the everyday qualities of competitive bridge. But, then, Paul Chemla is not an everyday player. Here he is in the annual match between France and Italy, living up yet again to José Le Dentu's description of him as the *enfant terrible* of French bridge.

Dealer South: E/W Vul.

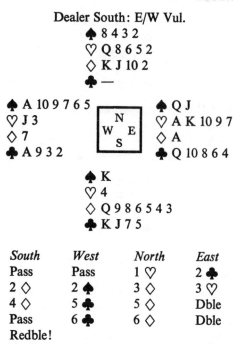

♠ 8 4 3 2
♡ Q 8 6 5 2
◇ K J 10 2
♣ —

♠ A 10 9 7 6 5   ♠ Q J
♡ J 3   ♡ A K 10 9 7
◇ 7   ◇ A
♣ A 9 3 2   ♣ Q 10 8 6 4

♠ K
♡ 4
◇ Q 9 8 6 5 4 3
♣ K J 7 5

South	West	North	East
Pass	Pass	1 ♡	2 ♣
2 ◇	2 ♠	3 ◇	3 ♡
4 ◇	5 ♣	5 ◇	Dble
Pass	6 ♣	6 ◇	Dble
Redble!			

Chemla was South. The bidding sequence would be unusual in a friendly rubber at home. In an international match it is unprecedented.

'Never before', said Blue Team star Walter Avarelli, who was East, 'have I doubled an opponent in 5 ◇ only to see him end up in 6 ◇ *redoubled!*'

Third hand, at favourable vulnerability, is the classic position for a psyche, a bluff bid designed to confuse opponents. Sometimes, as here, it confuses partner, too.

All would have been well, however, without Chemla's wanton redouble. A 500 penalty would have shown a profit, for East-West have an easy game.

Suspecting something from the bidding, Chemla should have realized that if he made his slam, he would have a good result anyway. To redouble was to daub the lily in the most garish hues.

How many tricks will declarer make here in 3 NT on a club lead?

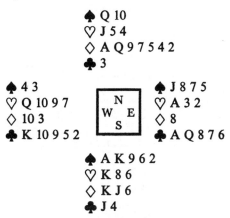

```
            ♠ Q 10
            ♡ J 5 4
            ◊ A Q 9 7 5 4 2
            ♣ 3

♠ 4 3                          ♠ J 8 7 5
♡ Q 10 9 7        N            ♡ A 3 2
◊ 10 3        W       E        ◊ 8
♣ K 10 9 5 2      S            ♣ A Q 8 7 6

            ♠ A K 9 6 2
            ♡ K 8 6
            ◊ K J 6
            ♣ J 4
```

The top pairs in France were locked in battle in the *sélection nationale*, the trials for the team to represent France in the European Championships.

The best game contract is 5 ◊. The second best is 4 ♠. The worst, by far, is 3 NT. Four of France's leading pairs found it, and strange to relate, one of them made twelve tricks—on a club lead!

East won the first trick with the ♣ A and returned ♣ 7. Convinced that declarer must have the queen behind the knave, West played low at trick two to preserve communications with partner. A startled declarer proceeded to make the rest. On the last diamond, the ninth card to be played, East had to part with a vital spade or to throw the ♡ A. Not only was the dog bitten, but he was squeezed too.

It is only fair to point out that it takes great players to have great catastrophes. Just as a mere abacus does not lend itself to the spectacular mistakes of the computer, so the ordinary player does not make such bold deductions as the master. How could the expert West visualize that the expert South had landed in so abominable a contract?

'Wrong views' are not the prerogative of the ordinary player. They are common at every level, though we hear more, of course, of the triumphs than of the tragedies that befall the stars. By way of a change, here's a 'wrong view' hand from the World Championship of 1974.

Dealer East: Both Vul.

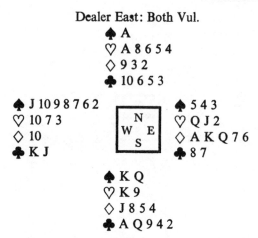

♠ A
♡ A 8 6 5 4
◇ 9 3 2
♣ 10 6 5 3

♠ J 10 9 8 7 6 2   ♠ 5 4 3
♡ 10 7 3   ♡ Q J 2
◇ 10   ◇ A K Q 7 6
♣ K J   ♣ 8 7

♠ K Q
♡ K 9
◇ J 8 5 4
♣ A Q 9 4 2

In one room the Italians went 800 down in a phantom 5 ♣ sacrifice against an unmakeable 4 ♠.

This is what happened in the other room, where Bob Hamman and Bobby Wolff, winners the previous week of the World Pairs Olympiad, sat North-South.

West	*North*	*East*	*South*
—	—	1 ◇	1 NT
3 ♠	3 NT		

Belladonna, West, led a spade. Needing all five tricks for his contract, Wolff, the declarer, took the double finesse in clubs, losing to the ♣ J. A second spade cleared the suit and now it was a question of going only one down.

Wolff crossed to the ♡ A and took a second club finesse. Five spades and three diamonds followed in quick succession—six down.

What an inquest there would have been had the hand occurred during the weekly duplicate at the local club!

What is the unlikeliest result on the unlikeliest contract for North-South? This is no Armenian riddle, but a hand from a Danish competition reported in the monthly *Bulletin* of the International Press Association.

Dealer East: Love All

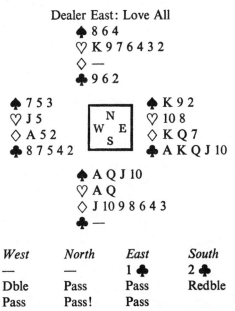

♠ 8 6 4
♥ K 9 7 6 4 3 2
♦ —
♣ 9 6 2

♠ 7 5 3   ♠ K 9 2
♥ J 5   ♥ 10 8
♦ A 5 2   ♦ K Q 7
♣ 8 7 5 4 2   ♣ A K Q J 10

♠ A Q J 10
♥ A Q
♦ J 10 9 8 6 4 3
♣ —

West	North	East	South
—	—	1 ♣	2 ♣
Dble	Pass	Pass	Redble
Pass	Pass!	Pass	

North assumed that the opening bid was a 'prepared' club and that South was showing clubs. He had never played with South before—and will doubtless not have the opportunity to do so again—and left in happily the anguished SOS redouble. Other considerations apart, it never occurred to him that thirteen diamonds must be lurking somewhere. If South had clubs, where were they?

Stranger even than that contract was the result. To play safe, West decided to look at the table and opened the ♦ A. Declarer ruffed in dummy, took the spade finesse, ruffed again and finessed in spades a second time. Another diamond ruff, the ♠ A and the two top hearts brought the total to eight tricks.

'A trump lead defeats the contract,' observed an earnest young kibitzer.

One of the biggest swings recorded in a world championship occurred on this deal in Venice in 1974.

Dealer South: N/S Vul.

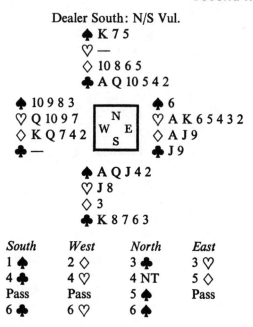

♠ K 7 5
♥ —
♦ 10 8 6 5
♣ A Q 10 5 4 2

♠ 10 9 8 3   ♠ 6
♥ Q 10 9 7   ♥ A K 6 5 4 3 2
♦ K Q 7 4 2   ♦ A J 9
♣ —   ♣ J 9

♠ A Q J 4 2
♥ J 8
♦ 3
♣ K 8 7 6 3

South	West	North	East
1 ♠	2 ♦	3 ♣	3 ♥
4 ♣	4 ♥	4 NT	5 ♦
Pass	Pass	5 ♠	Pass
6 ♣	6 ♥	6 ♠	

Such was the spirited auction when Italy's Belladonna sat
South and Garozzo, North. West led a heart allowing the Italians
to make all thirteen tricks.

In the other room, South doubled 6 ♥, another unbeatable
contract, and here, too, the defence started with the wrong ace,
presenting declarer with an overtrick. So Italy scored 1,430 in one
room and 1,310 in the other, a swing of 2,740 or 21 IMPs.

The hand is instructive as well as dramatic, bringing home the
wisdom of S. J. Simon's dictum on freak deals: 'when in doubt,
bid one more'.

Both sides rarely bid up to the six level unless one or other has
a void. Maybe both have voids, as here. Then it pays to bid on,
for aces cannot be relied upon to take tricks and it's worth
accepting a small loss to avoid a major disaster.

Would you bid a grand slam, voluntarily, knowing that an ace
was missing? It seems hardly possible, yet that was the bid made
with cold deliberation by Henri Svarc in the European Championships at Estoril.

Dealer West: N/S Vul.

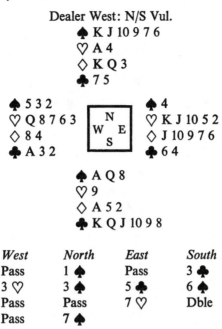

♠ K J 10 9 7 6
♡ A 4
◇ K Q 3
♣ 7 5

♠ 5 3 2
♡ Q 8 7 6 3
◇ 8 4
♣ A 3 2

♠ 4
♡ K J 10 5 2
◇ J 10 9 7 6
♣ 6 4

♠ A Q 8
♡ 9
◇ A 5 2
♣ K Q J 10 9 8

West	North	East	South
Pass	1 ♠	Pass	3 ♣
3 ♡	3 ♠	5 ♣	6 ♠
Pass	Pass	7 ♡	Dble
Pass	7 ♠		

Taking full advantage of the favourable vulnerability, world pairs champions, Babsch-Manhardt, sitting East-West for Austria, found an excellent sacrifice in 7 ♡. Svarc, North, had every reason to fear that an ace was missing. But it might be the ◇ A and the lead wouldn't necessarily be a diamond.

Should he accept the Austrian sacrifice for a penalty of 900, maybe less, or should he gamble on a grand slam? With his eyes wide open, Svarc went for the grand slam—and lost.

Though the French were worthy winners of the European Championships, they went down in the first seven grand slams they bid! Surely a record.

What would they say if that happened to you?

Everyone resents injustice. Brilliant defence defeats a game. Next hand opponents get a slam. A reckless overcall is rightly doubled. On a lucky lead and two finesses the contract is made. Bad luck, indeed. But good luck, too, can be frustrating. Recently I saw an expert play this hand.

Dealer South: Love All

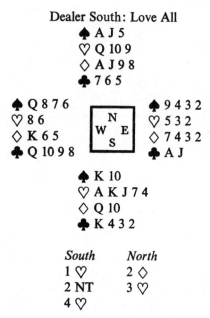

♠ A J 5
♡ Q 10 9
◇ A J 9 8
♣ 7 6 5

♠ Q 8 7 6　　　　　　　　　♠ 9 4 3 2
♡ 8 6　　　　　　　　　　　♡ 5 3 2
◇ K 6 5　　　　　　　　　　◇ 7 4 3 2
♣ Q 10 9 8　　　　　　　　♣ A J

♠ K 10
♡ A K J 7 4
◇ Q 10
♣ K 4 3 2

South	North
1 ♡	2 ◇
2 NT	3 ♡
4 ♡	

West led a trump and South looked for bad breaks. What if West had the ♣ A and East the ◇ K? South won in dummy and led the ♠ 5 to his ♠ 10, losing to West's ♠ Q. A second trump came back, but South was out of the wood. Dropping the ♠ K under the ♠ A, he discarded his ◇ Q on the ♠ J and continued with the ◇ A and ◇ J, taking the ruffing finesse. It lost, but with West on lead, the defence was powerless.

North was quick to point out that a less gifted declarer would have made twelve tricks in comfort. South could only plead that he had insured against bad breaks. Why should he be blamed for the good ones which he had done nothing to deserve?

Even in Man-Bites-Dog stories, dog shouldn't eat dog, so a discreet anonymity usually protects the wrongdoer. Truly great players, however, can well afford to tell stories against themselves. Bob Hamman has offered me this one.

Dealer West: Both Vul.

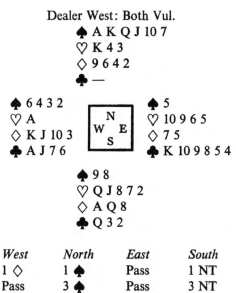

♠ A K Q J 10 7
♡ K 4 3
◇ 9 6 4 2
♣ —

♠ 6 4 3 2
♡ A
◇ K J 10 3
♣ A J 7 6

♠ 5
♡ 10 9 6 5
◇ 7 5
♣ K 10 9 8 5 4

♠ 9 8
♡ Q J 8 7 2
◇ A Q 8
♣ Q 3 2

West	North	East	South
1 ◇	1 ♠	Pass	1 NT
Pass	3 ♠	Pass	3 NT

West, a complete stranger, opened the ◇ J. Seeing eight tricks only, Bob Hamman, South, hoped to steal a heart. So he won the first trick cunningly with the ◇ A and led the ♡ J. West was intended to duck, but if not, to play a diamond, for surely East was 'marked' with the ◇ Q. Alas, West couldn't duck and he played, not a diamond, but a club. Maybe he wasn't good enough to be deceived. Maybe he was too good. Bob Hamman will never know. He went five down and never saw the stranger again.

Bad players get predictably bad results. For unpredictably bad results, one must look to the experts. Here is a hand from the Pairs Olympiad of 1970.

East is world champion, Billy Eisenberg, and West is the Californian star, Edwin Kantar.

Dealer West: N/S Vul.

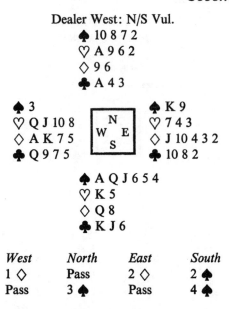

```
                ♠ 10 8 7 2
                ♡ A 9 6 2
                ◇ 9 6
                ♣ A 4 3
♠ 3                               ♠ K 9
♡ Q J 10 8          N            ♡ 7 4 3
◇ A K 7 5        W     E         ◇ J 10 4 3 2
♣ Q 9 7 5          S             ♣ 10 8 2
                ♠ A Q J 6 5 4
                ♡ K 5
                ◇ Q 8
                ♣ K J 6
```

West	North	East	South
1 ◇	Pass	2 ◇	2 ♠
Pass	3 ♠	Pass	4 ♠

The lead was the ♡ Q. Winning in dummy, South played a diamond to his queen, which Kantar captured cleverly with the ◇ A. Why? Because he wanted declarer to think that East had the ◇ K. Then he would place West, on his opening bid, with a trump honour and misplay the hand accordingly. Of course, only an expert could think so far ahead.

At trick three, Kantar returned a low diamond and it was Eisenberg's turn to show expertise. Knowing that South had only one diamond left—the ◇ K, 'naturally'—he played low to give Kantar a count on the suit.

South, the Danish champion, Moller, gathered the unexpected gift and reeled off six trumps, squeezing Kantar in hearts and clubs for twelve tricks and a cold top.

The story is told by Kantar himself in *The Bridge World.*

As well as being one of America's best players, Eddie Kantar is one of her most successful teachers. Even he, however, cannot win all the time. The diagrammed hand fitted well into one of my week-end quizzes.

Dealer East: Love All

♠ 8 3
♡ J 10 7
◇ 10 8 6
♣ A K J 10 5

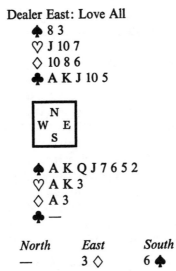

♠ A K Q J 7 6 5 2
♡ A K 3
◇ A 3
♣ —

West	North	East	South
West	*North*	*East*	*South*
—	—	3 ◇	6 ♠

West leads the ◇ 2 to East's ◇ J. Declarer wins and lays down the ♠ A. East discards the ◇ 4.

How should declarer play to make certain of his contract?

The ◇ 2 can only be a singleton, so that if West can be thrown in he will have to lead a heart or a club and either will enable declarer to get at dummy's ♣ A K.

After cashing two top spades, South uses his most valuable card, the ♠ 2, to put West on play. West can try to unblock by throwing his ♠ 10 9 on South's ♠ A K, but he remains with the ♠ 4, a fatal liability.

♠ 10 9 4   ♠ —
♡ Q 9 8 4   ♡ 6 5 2
◇ 2   ◇ K Q J 9 7 5 4
♣ 9 8 7 6 4   ♣ Q 3 2

This is a hand often used in his lessons by Eddie Kantar. Only a few advanced players get it right, but one beginner at a practice class quickly floored him.

After drawing trumps, she led dummy's ♣ A. No one stopped her, so she made all thirteen tricks.

'What's the problem?' she asked.

There's a fascination about freaks—wild distributions, sensational swings and topsy-turvy results.

The *reductio ad absurdum* is reached on 1st April when it is safe to predict that someone, somewhere, will hold a complete suit. The odds against it, which any reader can, of course, easily check, have been computed by the mathematician, Rouse Ball at 53,644,737,756,488,792,839,237,440,000 to 1. Yet it keeps happening and not only on the 1st April.

Imperfect shuffling makes nonsense of the odds, but the wildest freaks of all come up in goulashes—a method of dealing, without shuffling, three, four or five cards at a time. A goulash is usually introduced after a hand has been passed out.

A memorable goulash is on record at Crockfords. Sitting south, in a big money game, was one of Britain's most gifted players. He picked up:

```
      ┌─────────┐
      │    N    │
      │ W     E │
      │    S    │
      └─────────┘
```

♠ —
♡ K Q J 10 9 8 7 6 5 4 3 2
◇ A
♣ —

West, in front of him, opened 5 ◇, North bid 6 ♣ and East 7 ♠. Placing him with thirteen spades, South bid boldly 7 NT. Not only would he rob East of his grand slam, but he, South, would score one himself. North, he reasoned, must have the two missing aces. A diamond would be opened—West, of course, had no spades—and South would throw it on dummy's singleton ♡ A, unblocking his twelve-card suit. A glorious vision.

East doubled and West duly led a diamond, but dummy, alas, had no ♡ A. East had it, together with twelve spades. So South won the first trick, but no other. And East, it transpired, would have gone down in 7 ♠, for North had a spade and would have ruffed a heart at trick one. Such things are not uncommon after goulashes.

Though one or two clubs in London have them, goulashes are almost unknown outside France. In Paris, however, they have a distinct following, with Pierre Jaïs as one of the leading exponents.

More than once, readers have asked me what the correct bid would be with thirteen cards of a suit. An example of what not to do comes from Paris. The deal was, of course, a goulash.

Dealer East: Both Vul.

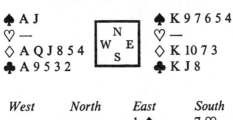

♠ A J
♡ —
◇ A Q J 8 5 4
♣ A 9 5 3 2

♠ K 9 7 6 5 4
♡ —
◇ K 10 7 3
♣ K J 8

West	North	East	South
—	—	1 ♠	7 ♡
7 NT			

The immediate jump to 7 ♡ isn't very subtle, and holding three aces, West can easily deduce that South must have all thirteen hearts. Against that West has no defence and any likely penalty will show a big profit. So he is only too willing to sacrifice. But when dummy goes down, the question arises: with every card marked by South's revealing bid, need it be a sacrifice?

North leads a diamond. Winning in his hand, declarer finesses the ♣ 8. Back in his hand with a diamond, he finesses the ♣ J and cashes the ♣ K. Another diamond takes him back to the closed hand, and after cashing the ♣ A, he reels off the rest of the diamonds. When he comes to the last one, dummy remains with ♠ K 9 7 6, while North must find a discard from ♠ Q 10 8 ♣ Q. He is helpless.

West's thirteenth trick will be either his ♣ 9 or dummy's ♠ 9.

By and large, experts tend to pass cunningly the first time round on wild freaks. It isn't always a success. An example is this hand from a match between France and Brazil in Rio in 1961.

Dealer South: Game All

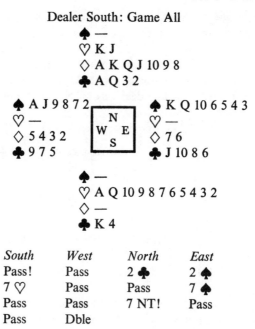

♠ —
♡ K J
◇ A K Q J 10 9 8
♣ A Q 3 2

♠ A J 9 8 7 2
♡ —
◇ 5 4 3 2
♣ 9 7 5

♠ K Q 10 6 5 4 3
♡ —
◇ 7 6
♣ J 10 8 6

♠ —
♡ A Q 10 9 8 7 6 5 4 3 2
◇ —
♣ K 4

South	West	North	East
Pass!	Pass	2 ♣	2 ♠
7 ♡	Pass	Pass	7 ♠
Pass	Pass	7 NT!	Pass
Pass	Dble		

After South's cunning pass, both he and North had to bid with their eyes shut. North's 7 NT isn't as outrageous as it appears. It didn't occur to him that South also had a void in spades, and since he bid 7 ♡ over 2 ♠, he simply had to have the ♠ A. This was logical, but it cost 2,000 just the same.

In the other room, Brazil's South opened 2 ♣ and Roger Trézel, West, one of Europe's greatest players, bid a psychic 2 ♡. This didn't prevent North-South from reaching 7 ♡, but it effectively deterred East from bidding spades.

The swing to Brazil was 4,210, nearly—but not quite—enough to win the match.

A recent experiment with the goulash in America, where it is virtually unknown, led to the curious situation on the diagrammed hand, reported from Dallas by world champion, Bobby Wolff.

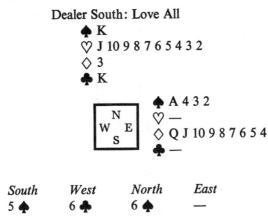

Dealer South: Love All

♠ K
♡ J 10 9 8 7 6 5 4 3 2
◇ 3
♣ K

♠ A 4 3 2
♡ —
◇ Q J 10 9 8 7 6 5 4
♣ —

South	West	North	East
South	*West*	*North*	*East*
5 ♠	6 ♣	6 ♠	—

South's 5 ♠ opening shows that he is interested only in trumps. With one top honour, North calls 6 ♠. With two (♠ A K) he would bid 7 ♠. West leads the ♣ A. How can East make certain of beating the contract?

If East works out South's hand, he has the answer. Since South cannot have a loser outside trumps, he is marked with a void in clubs. And his red cards must all be tops.

So East ruffs the ♣ A with the ♠ A and leads a diamond. Though South has only winners left, the trumps are blocked in dummy and he cannot get back to draw them without playing a heart which East promptly ruffs. Ninety-nine Wests out of a hundred would have sacrificed in 7 ♣, but that's neither here nor there.

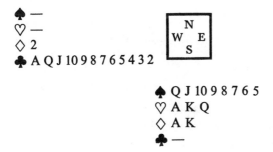

♠ —
♡ —
◇ 2
♣ A Q J 10 9 8 7 6 5 4 3 2

♠ Q J 10 9 8 7 6 5
♡ A K Q
◇ A K
♣ —

A freak of freaks came up in 1970 at the Canterbury Bridge Club. The reader, who sent me the hand, sat South with:

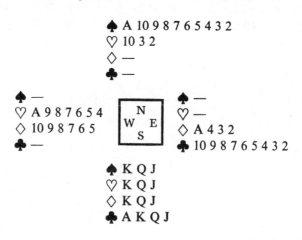

♠ K Q J
♡ K Q J
◇ K Q J
♣ A K Q J

Regretting that he wasn't playing rubber bridge for high stakes and wondering how to make the best of his picture gallery, his thoughts were rudely interrupted by North, the dealer, who opened proceedings with 4 ♠.

What should South do now? There was no precedent, for surely no one had ever held a 28-point hand opposite an opening bid before. A Blackwood enquiry for aces was the obvious step and South's lips were shaping for the 'four' sound, when East burst through the bidding barrier with 6 ♣. Since two aces could be missing, South doubled, collecting 900—and the roundest of zeros. Two aces were, indeed, missing, but North would have made thirteen tricks just the same. This was the full deal.

                    ♠ A 10 9 8 7 6 5 4 3 2
                    ♡ 10 3 2
                    ◇ —
                    ♣ —

    ♠ —   ♠ —
    ♡ A 9 8 7 6 5 4   N   ♡ —
    ◇ 10 9 8 7 6 5   W   E   ◇ A 4 3 2
    ♣ —   S   ♣ 10 9 8 7 6 5 4 3 2

                    ♠ K Q J
                    ♡ K Q J
                    ◇ K Q J
                    ♣ A K Q J

North	East	South	West
4 ♠	6 ♣	Dble	

One must sympathize with South, but with wild freaks about it is generally wise to keep on bidding. A misguess may still lead to a zero, but somehow it isn't so round.

For the next curiosity we go back to Paris. The reader may like to treat the hand as a double-dummy problem.

After the bidding indicated below, West leads the ♣ K against South's 4 ♡. How should declarer set out to make his contract?

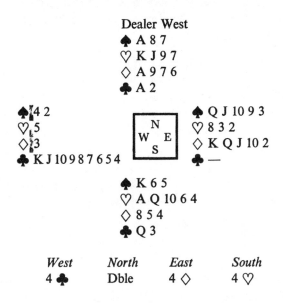

Dealer West
♠ A 8 7
♡ K J 9 7
◇ A 9 7 6
♣ A 2

♠ 4 2
♡ 5
◇ 3
♣ K J 10 9 8 7 6 5 4

♠ Q J 10 9 3
♡ 8 3 2
◇ K Q J 10 2
♣ —

♠ K 6 5
♡ A Q 10 6 4
◇ 8 5 4
♣ Q 3

West	North	East	South
4 ♣	Dble	4 ◇	4 ♡

This is what happened.

West opened the ♣ K, and as East ruffed dummy's ace, the kibitzers exchanged meaning glances. Then, as South threw his ♣ Q under East's trump, they gasped, for the play, though spectacular, made no sense.

Winning the spade return with his king, declarer drew trumps, cashed the ◇ A, then the ♠ A. West, who had clubs only left, was thrown in with a club and forced to lead another. South discarded a spade from dummy and a diamond from his hand.

West, still on lead, had to play another club. This time, South took advantage of the ruff and discard, ruffing in dummy and discarding the last diamond from his hand. He was home.

Modestly disclaiming all credit for his brilliant play, South explained that he had recognized a situation presented as a problem in *Le Bridgeur* some years earlier. Turning over his files, a correspondent found the original. The ♣ A 2 had faced the ♣ K 3 and declarer had to throw the king under the ace, but the point of the play was identical. A double-dummy problem had come to life.

Once again the reader may like to study the complete deal and play double-dummy. The hand came up in a pairs event at the Savoy Club in Los Angeles.

Dealer South: Love All

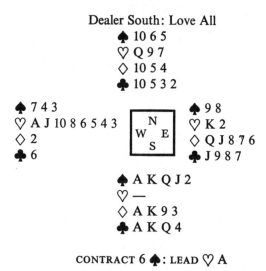

CONTRACT 6 ♠: LEAD ♡ A

How should South play?

This is the solution. South ruffs high, draws trumps, ending in dummy and ruffs a second heart, dropping East's ♡ K. South and East remain with four cards in each minor—and now comes the key card—the ◇ 9. If East wins, he cannot avoid leading up to dummy's ◇ 10 or ♣ 10 and South discards his other loser on the ♡ Q. If East allows the ◇ 9 to hold, declarer cashes the

◇ A K and throws East in with his last diamond, compelling a club return.

Grand slams and huge penalties have an understandable allure —so long as one isn't at the receiving end. Marshall Miles, one of America's leading writers and rubber bridge players sat West on this hand, reported in *Popular Bridge*.

Dealer West: Game All

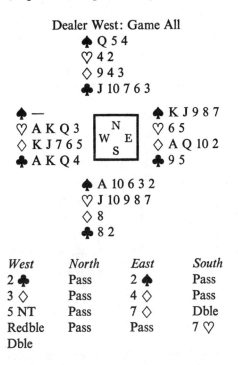

```
              ♠ Q 5 4
              ♡ 4 2
              ◇ 9 4 3
              ♣ J 10 7 6 3

  ♠ —                        ♠ K J 9 8 7
  ♡ A K Q 3      N           ♡ 6 5
  ◇ K J 7 6 5  W   E         ◇ A Q 10 2
  ♣ A K Q 4      S           ♣ 9 5

              ♠ A 10 6 3 2
              ♡ J 10 9 8 7
              ◇ 8
              ♣ 8 2
```

West	North	East	South
2 ♣	Pass	2 ♠	Pass
3 ◇	Pass	4 ◇	Pass
5 NT	Pass	7 ◇	Dble
Redble	Pass	Pass	7 ♡
Dble			

Marshall Miles, West, had no problems. Once partner supported diamonds, it only remained to apply the 5 NT grand slam force, asking him to bid 7 ◇ if he had two of the three top honours.

South doubled to ensure a spade lead, but the redouble told him what he must have feared all along, that Marshall Miles had no spades. Against 2,610, the price of 7 ◇ redoubled, 7 ♡ looked cheap.

Marshall Miles opened the ♡ Q, continued with two top clubs

and then the ♣ 4, which East ruffed and South over-ruffed. No matter what happened now, declarer could only win one more trick.

North maintains to this day that a more inspired player would have gone only ten down.

From money bridge we go to a teams-of-four match with IMPs as the currency.

A difference of 4,000 points in a match is converted to 24 IMPs. That is the maximum and it is almost as great a rarity as picking up a complete suit. A spectacular deal in a New England Tournament produced such a swing, the same team scoring a doubled small slam in one room and a doubled grand slam in the other.

Dealer South: Both Vul.

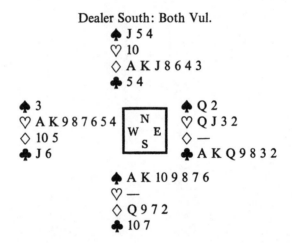

```
                   ♠ J 5 4
                   ♡ 10
                   ◇ A K J 8 6 4 3
                   ♣ 5 4
♠ 3                                      ♠ Q 2
♡ A K 9 8 7 6 5 4   ┌─────────┐          ♡ Q J 3 2
◇ 10 5              │    N    │          ◇ —
♣ J 6              │ W     E │          ♣ A K Q 9 8 3 2
                   │    S    │
                   └─────────┘
                   ♠ A K 10 9 8 7 6
                   ♡ —
                   ◇ Q 9 7 2
                   ♣ 10 7
```

In one room, North-South reached 6 ♠, after a keenly-contested auction in which diamonds had been bid and supported. East made a Lightner lead-directing double and duly ruffed a diamond at trick one. A club return leads to an 800 penalty. East, however, led a heart. So the slam was made for a score of 1,660.

In the other room, East-West bid 7 ♡, doubled by North. Having heard his partner open the bidding with 4 ♠, North decided on a 'safe' opening and led the ◇ A. Declarer spread his hand, scoring 2,470.

It is worthy of note that the losers, Alvin Roth's team from New York, went on to win the match!

The late Al Sobel, one of the great tournament directors of our time, was an ardent collector of curios. This one from a tournament in New Orleans, was a prize piece.

Dealer East
♠ J 9 4
♡ A Q 2
♢ K Q 10 8 6
♣ K 3

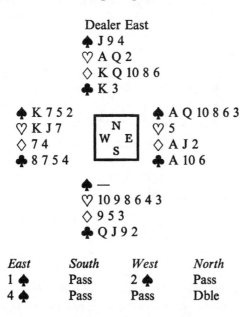

♠ K 7 5 2   ♠ A Q 10 8 6 3
♡ K J 7   ♡ 5
♢ 7 4   ♢ A J 2
♣ 8 7 5 4   ♣ A 10 6

♠ —
♡ 10 9 8 6 4 3
♢ 9 5 3
♣ Q J 9 2

East	South	West	North
1 ♠	Pass	2 ♠	Pass
4 ♠	Pass	Pass	Dble

What made North double isn't altogether clear, but the contract was, in fact, defeated. The remarkable part of the hand, however, is that North, the doubler, did not win a single trick for the defence. All four were taken by South!

This is how the play went. South opened the ♣ Q and was allowed to hold the trick. He switched to the ♡ 10 and that, too, held. Next came the ♣ 2 to the king and ace. Declarer drew three rounds of trumps, finishing in his hand, and continued with a low diamond towards dummy. South went up with the ♢ 9 and again held the trick, his third. Now he cashed the ♣ J to beat the contract, all on his own, as it were.

Very odd, yet no one did anything out of the way or played badly.

It's rare to make a slam against three opposing aces. It's rarer still, having done so, to complain of bad luck. This, however, is what happened to French international, Henri Bacherich, who was South here:

Dealer West: E/W Vul.

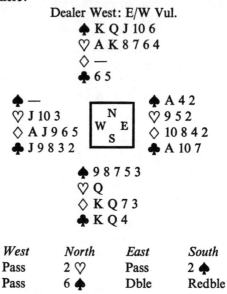

```
                    ♠ K Q J 10 6
                    ♡ A K 8 7 6 4
                    ◇ —
                    ♣ 6 5

  ♠ —                              ♠ A 4 2
  ♡ J 10 3          N              ♡ 9 5 2
  ◇ A J 9 6 5    W     E           ◇ 10 8 4 2
  ♣ J 9 8 3 2       S              ♣ A 10 7

                    ♠ 9 8 7 5 3
                    ♡ Q
                    ◇ K Q 7 3
                    ♣ K Q 4
```

West	North	East	South
Pass	2 ♡	Pass	2 ♠
Pass	6 ♠	Dble	Redble

The ♡ J is led. How can South make 6 ♠ ?

He wins in hand, ruffs a diamond and discards two clubs on the ♡ A K. Next comes another heart which East ruffs low to prevent South from discarding his third club.

South over-ruffs, ruffs another diamond and again leads a heart. Once more East ruffs and South over-ruffs. A third diamond is ruffed and dummy's last heart follows. Whether or not East ruffs with the ♠ A, declarer throws his third club.

Bacherich made his contract. Why, then, the bad luck? Because West led, not the ♡ J, but the ◇ A. Now all South had to do was to ruff and discard dummy's clubs on the ◇ K Q. Too easy. An 'unlucky' lead had robbed declarer of the chance to execute a rare coup, called by the French *Le Coup de l'Agonie*.

The impossible isn't as unusual as it's often made out to be. Both the deals below have been authenticated.

'Tournament Director!' called North. According to the travelling score-sheet, a North-South pair had made an over-trick in 6 ♡ doubled. Impossible. The Tournament Director investigated, but no, the score had been entered correctly. This is what happened.

Dealer West: Both Vul.

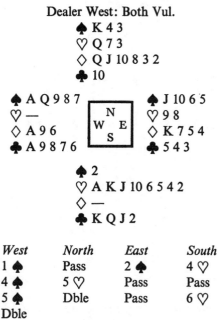

```
                    ♠ K 4 3
                    ♡ Q 7 3
                    ◊ Q J 10 8 3 2
                    ♣ 10
  ♠ A Q 9 8 7                    ♠ J 10 6 5
  ♡ —              N             ♡ 9 8
  ◊ A 9 6       W     E          ◊ K 7 5 4
  ♣ A 9 8 7 6      S             ♣ 5 4 3
                    ♠ 2
                    ♡ A K J 10 6 5 4 2
                    ◊ —
                    ♣ K Q J 2
```

West	North	East	South
1 ♠	Pass	2 ♠	4 ♡
4 ♠	5 ♡	Pass	Pass
5 ♠	Dble	Pass	6 ♡
Dble			

What should West lead? He placed South with a void somewhere, probably in spades, but maybe in clubs. A diamond opening looked safest, but which one? The ◊ A might help to set up dummy's side suit and West wasn't playing for just one down. After deep thought, he picked the ◊ 6, hoping to confuse declarer without giving anything away.

South went up with dummy's ◊ Q and East played low, for which no one could blame him. Declarer discarded his ♠ 2, took two rounds of trumps and continued with the ♣ 2. Fearing to go up with the ♣ A, in case it cost a trick, maybe even two, West played the ♣ 9—and it only remained for South to get back with a diamond ruff and lead clubs till West covered.

A different scenario, but the same overture. Once more North opens the travelling score-sheet and sends for the Tournament Director. 'This is nonsense,' he cries, 'we can't make ten tricks, let alone thirteen.' But the result had been recorded correctly.

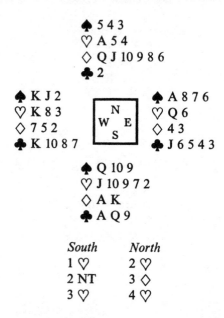

```
              ♠ 5 4 3
              ♡ A 5 4
              ◇ Q J 10 9 8 6
              ♣ 2
♠ K J 2                         ♠ A 8 7 6
♡ K 8 3          N              ♡ Q 6
◇ 7 5 2      W       E          ◇ 4 3
♣ K 10 8 7       S              ♣ J 6 5 4 3
              ♠ Q 10 9
              ♡ J 10 9 7 2
              ◇ A K
              ♣ A Q 9
```

South	North
1 ♡	2 ♡
2 NT	3 ◇
3 ♡	4 ♡

Deducing from the bidding that dummy would have ruffing value, West opened a trump, and to give nothing away, he chose the deceptive ♡ 8. Declarer played low from dummy and East, duly deceived, played low, too. Why should he waste the ♡ Q?

Winning with the ♡ 10, South laid down the ◇ A K, and continued with the ♡ J. West 'knew' that declarer must have the ♡ Q, since East hadn't produced it at trick one, so he covered, his ♡ K colliding ignominiously under the ace with East's ♡ Q. Dummy's ♡ 5 was good enough to draw West's ♡ 3, the last outstanding trump, and thereafter came the diamonds. Defenders signalled madly in the black suits, putting each other off to put off declarer. Clever to the end, West bared both his kings, and the ♣ A Q won the last two tricks. The kibitzers are still debating whether against the best defence South can make nine tricks.

Unlike some games which spring to mind, bridge is essentially civilized and there is no record of a tournament director being lynched. A ruling from a pairs event in North Carolina might have set a precedent.

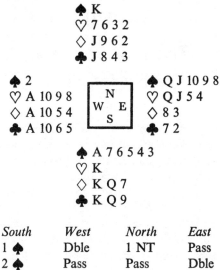

```
                    ♠ K
                    ♡ 7 6 3 2
                    ◇ J 9 6 2
                    ♣ J 8 4 3
♠ 2                                    ♠ Q J 10 9 8
♡ A 10 9 8          N                  ♡ Q J 5 4
◇ A 10 5 4      W       E              ◇ 8 3
♣ A 10 6 5          S                  ♣ 7 2
                    ♠ A 7 6 5 4 3
                    ♡ K
                    ◇ K Q 7
                    ♣ K Q 9
```

South	West	North	East
1 ♠	Dble	1 NT	Pass
2 ♠	Pass	Pass	Dble

West led the ♠ 2 to dummy's ♠ K. A heart to the ♡ K followed, unleashing a chain reaction of farce and tragedy. Having mixed up his red aces, West 'won' the ♡ K with the ◇ A and promptly laid down the ♣ A.

'Tournament Director!' cried South.

The Director ruled that the ◇ A had been played, establishing a revoke and that the ♣ A was an exposed card. South thereupon led the ♠ A, picking up the ♣ A and cashed the ♣ K Q and ◇ K Q, now masters. East couldn't be deprived of three trump tricks, but two of them had to be transferred to declarer to pay for the revoke. South ended up with twelve tricks, including four doubled overtricks.

Sometime I will show you the rest of my files, but not now, for here goes the bell, recalling us to the auditorium.

ACT III

The money motif

cash before cups

As the curtain goes up we see the same scenery as before. The same heroes and villains appear before the footlights and most of them still speak their lines in Italian. Yet something has changed and the orchestra is playing a new tune.

In years of yore, players thirsted for honour and glory. The quest for the holy grail led to the Bermuda Bowl, while on the national plane the keen young player's greatest ambition was to represent his country in the European Championships.

Travelling abroad was an expensive business and there was no money in it at the end of the road.

A few, a very few, prospered through bridge. Culbertson and Goren made fortunes, and a sprinkling of teachers earned a living. But, by and large, there was no incentive to take up the game professionally.

This is changing. Sponsored promotions are transforming the scene, and though it is too early to see the shape of things to come, one thing is certain: commercialism has invaded bridge, as it has invaded—and conquered—other games, and things will never be the same again. That is why the orchestra is playing a different tune.

The young, even the Italian young, must still prove their worth and international tournaments provide the only testing ground. But the superstars are no longer drawn, as of old, to world and European events. Having won their laurels, they can now win money.

Before there was no money to win. Now there is.

Only two members of the *squadra azzurra* competed for the Bowl in 1975. Only one played in that year's European Championships in Brighton. Yet four of the invincibles, Belladonna and Avarelli, Forquet and Garozzo, the greatest of the great, did battle for Omar's Lancia-sponsored team that summer in the United States.

As commercialism gains ground, so cups and trophies yield precedence to cash.

All this didn't happen overnight. It was a gradual process and it would be hard to draw a dividing line. Money prizes, severely frowned upon by the British and American Bridge Leagues, had been creeping in for years through the back door.

Valuable watches and bejewelled vanity cases had long been among the attractions for bridge events at St. Moritz in the winter and Deauville in the summer. Cash prizes, too, were to be won in France, in Spain and in Portugal. The municipalities and the hotels were the earliest sponsors, but the rewards till recently were too modest to lend a commercial flavour to what were primarily holidays in the sun.

Year by year the prizes grew in value—a fortnight's holiday, a cruise, a car. Then, shedding all inhibitions, promoters offered crisp thousand franc notes and worth-while cheques.

One of the first tournaments with big prizes was the *Cino de Duca* Pairs, named after the Italian publisher and philanthropist. In 1970 four Renault cars—readily convertible into currency—were offered to the winners and runners-up.

Only just pipped at the post that year were Britain's Martin Hoffman and Paul Hackett. This hand is interesting as an example of match-point technique.

Dealer South: Love All

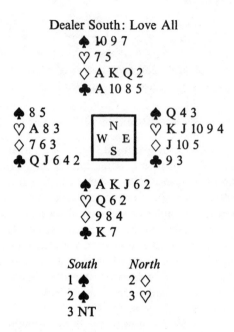

```
            ♠ 10 9 7
            ♡ 7 5
            ◇ A K Q 2
            ♣ A 10 8 5
♠ 8 5                        ♠ Q 4 3
♡ A 8 3        N            ♡ K J 10 9 4
◇ 7 6 3     W     E         ◇ J 10 5
♣ Q J 6 4 2    S            ♣ 9 3
            ♠ A K J 6 2
            ♡ Q 6 2
            ◇ 9 8 4
            ♣ K 7
```

South	*North*
1 ♠	2 ◇
2 ♠	3 ♡
3 NT	

Hackett, South, knew that 4 ♠ would be superior to 3 NT, but 630 against 620 could make all the difference, for in match-point scoring the pair that does best wins most. How much better it does than the next pair is immaterial.

Hackett won the diamond lead in dummy, took the finesse in spades and cashed his nine winners. To keep a guard in clubs, West bared his ♡ A. When Hackett threw him in with it, he exited with the ♣ Q, and the finesse against the ♣ J yielded declarer a twelfth trick, a cold top. West should have played a low club, but it would have made no difference for no other pair had scored 460.

Organizer of the tournament was Pierre Jaïs, holder of three world titles. Though he couldn't compete in his own event, he brought off that year a remarkable coup in the trials to select the French team which won the European and went on to meet the Aces for the world title at Taipeh.

Dealer South: Love All

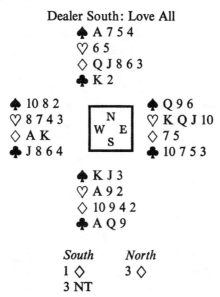

♠ A 7 5 4
♡ 6 5
◇ Q J 8 6 3
♣ K 2

♠ 10 8 2   ♠ Q 9 6
♡ 8 7 4 3   ♡ K Q J 10
◇ A K   ◇ 7 5
♣ J 8 6 4   ♣ 10 7 5 3

♠ K J 3
♡ A 9 2
◇ 10 9 4 2
♣ A Q 9

South	*North*
1 ◇	3 ◇
3 NT	

West opened the ♠ 2. Jaïs played low from dummy and followed to East's ♠ Q with the ♠ 3! Going up confidently with the ♡ A on the heart switch, Jaïs led a diamond to West's ◇ K. The spade return was taken in dummy with the ♠ A, Jaïs dropping the ♠ J, and a second diamond cleared the suit. Bemused, bothered and bewildered, poor West played back a spade, for who but East could have the ♠ K?

By 1973 all seven veils had been discarded and everywhere on the Continent competitors were offered money in the nude.

A double prize list, with more than 40,000 dollars in cash, was a feature of the International Bridge Festival at the Sheraton Hotel in Brussels. One prize list was open to all. The other was reserved for non-experts.

The organizer was Tony Trad, a regular member of the Swiss team. This hand, from the *Sunday Times* Pairs, illustrates his skill as a card-player.

Dealer West: N/S Vul.

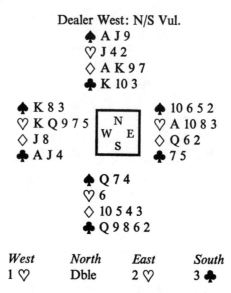

♠ A J 9
♡ J 4 2
◇ A K 9 7
♣ K 10 3

♠ K 8 3
♡ K Q 9 7 5
◇ J 8
♣ A J 4

♠ 10 6 5 2
♡ A 10 8 3
◇ Q 6 2
♣ 7 5

♠ Q 7 4
♡ 6
◇ 10 5 4 3
♣ Q 9 8 6 2

West	North	East	South
1 ♡	Dble	2 ♡	3 ♣

Hearts were led. South ruffed and led the ♠ Q, covered by the ♠ K and ♠ A. Ruffing dummy's last heart, South lost a second spade finesse to East's ♠ 10 and was put back to dummy with the ♠ J.

Once more on play after three rounds of diamonds, East exited with the thirteenth spade, ruffed with the ♣ 8 by South, over-ruffed by Trad with the ♣ J and won in dummy.

With three cards left, each hand had two trumps. The eleventh trick was made up of dummy's ♣ 3, East's ♣ 5, South's ♣ 9 and Trad's—♣ 4!

Declarer was helpless. If he led the ♣ Q, the defence would make a heart. If he led a diamond, East would score his ♣ 7.

In glamour and excitement no event at present compares with the Monte Carlo Tournament, launched the same year by French international, Jean-Michel Boulenger. With more than 60,000 dollars to be won, it attracted leading players from both sides of the Atlantic and enjoyed more publicity than the World Championship itself, which preceded it by a fortnight or so.

My first Monte Carlo hand was:

Dealer South: Love All

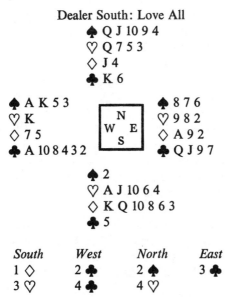

♠ Q J 10 9 4
♡ Q 7 5 3
◇ J 4
♣ K 6

♠ A K 5 3   ♠ 8 7 6
♡ K   ♡ 9 8 2
◇ 7 5   ◇ A 9 2
♣ A 10 8 4 3 2   ♣ Q J 9 7

♠ 2
♡ A J 10 6 4
◇ K Q 10 8 6 3
♣ 5

South	West	North	East
1 ◇	2 ♣	2 ♠	3 ♣
3 ♡	4 ♣	4 ♡	

West leads the ♠ K, then the ♣ A and continues with the ♠.A.

As declarer sees it, the contract hinges on picking up the ♡ K. The finesse is mandatory, but dummy's only possible entry is the ◇ J, and when East produces the ◇ A, declarer is forced to lay down the ♡ A and drop the bare ♡ K.

After ruffing the ♠ A, most declarers led a low diamond, hoping to find West with the ◇ A.

When Nicola Gardener, then aged twenty-four and our youngest Life Master, made that play, she had the ill-fortune to find Edwin Kantar sitting East.

Eddie could see why, instead of drawing trumps, Nicola was trying to get to dummy. Evidently she wanted to take the trump finesse. So he would let her take it. Smoothly Eddie followed to the ◇ J with the ◇ 2! Of course, at this table, though at no other, the ♡ K made a trick.

Meanwhile, unnoticed in a blaze of publicity, the money motif scored a significant success on the more lofty moral plane.

As to the American Contract Bridge League, so to the British, cash prizes had always been anathema. IMPs, match-points and master points were pure. Money wasn't. It tended to corrupt, to lower ethical standards, and ever present was the danger of collusion between competitors who might arrange to give each other tops and subsequently share the money.

None of these exalted considerations applied when the British Bridge League set out to raise a £25,000 fund to finance the 1975 European Championships in Brighton.

Ladbrokes, leaders in the world of gaming and bookmaking, were the Fund's first and biggest benefactors. Over £700 was raised by their first venture—a contest in which every pair consisted of an expert and an amateur. As in the Jewish National Fund competition, there was a spirited auction for the chances of each pair, one or two fetching £500.

Then came a tournament, unique in more ways than one. Twenty players of renown paid £100 each to enter an Individual with a first prize of £2,000. Again there was a sweepstake, heavy betting on the result and a substantial contribution to the BBL Fund.

Omar Sharif was the very popular winner. My hand for the occasion featured Pietro Bernasconi, sitting East here.

♠ K 10 8 6 4
♡ 6 5
◇ 4
♣ A K 8 6 5

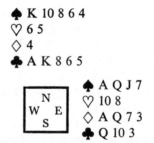

♠ A Q J 7
♡ 10 8
◇ A Q 7 3
♣ Q 10 3

South deals and bids 4 ♡. All pass. West leads the ♡ 3. Declarer wins and plays the ♣ 2, ducking in dummy. East is in. What should he return?

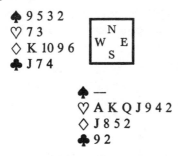

♠ 9 5 3 2
♡ 7 3
◇ K 10 9 6
♣ J 7 4

♠ —
♡ A K Q J 9 4 2
◇ J 8 5 2
♣ 9 2

Bernasconi immediately played back another club, cutting declarer's communications with dummy, the only defence to beat the contract.

While, at Ladbrokes, Omar was fighting off Bee Schenken—a 66–1 chance—who had taken an early lead, commercialism was winning a battle at sea.

In America, bridge cruises had been big business for years. On British ships, bridge teachers were sometimes part of the entertainment, like conjurers, drummers or dancing masters—'performing seals' as one of them, Nico Gardener, was wont to call them. Bridge was a service, one of many, not worth mentioning in advertisements, catalogues or brochures.

The idea that organized bridge, with celebrities on board, could attract hundreds of passengers, hadn't occurred to anyone. It was born at the 1972 *Evening Standard* Charity Bridge Congress, when P & O agreed to give me a fortnight's cruise as the first prize. Richard Esdale, then P & O's Promotions Manager, thought that something more could be made of it and invited me to try. I did, and the following June, Britain's first 'Bridge Congress Afloat' sailed on *Oriana* to Athens, Istanbul and the Black Sea, with more than two hundred bridge enthusiasts on board.

We had lessons and lectures every morning, for advanced players and for beginners alike, rubber bridge throughout the day and duplicate pairs in the evening. And in port, we played matches against Greek, Turkish and Portuguese teams, who welcomed us to their clubs and were, in turn, welcomed on board.

In Athens, we were televised in a pairs event, organized especially for Greece's younger players.

Honor Flint and I, the fortunate winners, badly needed a good score when we met our team-mates, Jeremy Flint and Nico Gardener.

Dealer West: Love All

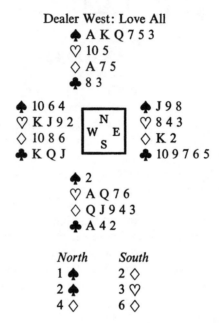

♠ A K Q 7 5 3
♡ 10 5
◇ A 7 5
♣ 8 3

♠ 10 6 4
♡ K J 9 2
◇ 10 8 6
♣ K Q J

♠ J 9 8
♡ 8 4 3
◇ K 2
♣ 10 9 7 6 5

♠ 2
♡ A Q 7 6
◇ Q J 9 4 3
♣ A 4 2

North	*South*
1 ♠	2 ◇
2 ♠	3 ♡
4 ◇	6 ◇

Bearing in mind the mechanics of match-point scoring, with its heavy bias in favour of no trumps, I would have done better to bid 3 NT over Honor Flint's 2 ♠. Once we had passed the point of no return, however, I had to bid the slam, for a mere 400 in 5 ◇ would have been a wretched result against other Souths scoring 430 or 460.

West led the ♣ K and now everything had to be right. After parking two clubs on dummy's spades, I led a low diamond from dummy. Jeremy Flint followed nonchalantly with the ◇ 2, but I couldn't go wrong.

A spectacular success, the 'Congress Afloat' was quickly followed by others and in 1975 the Norwegian-America Line invited me to organize bridge for every cruise on their all-first-class *Vistafjord*, surely the most luxurious ship in the world.

Two cruises were special bridge promotions.

I ended every lecture with a quiz, presenting the problem one day, the solution the next. This was one of them.

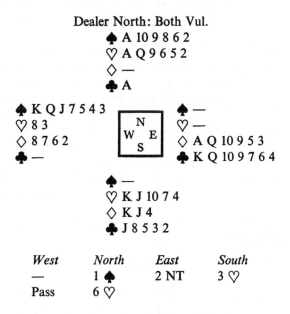

Dealer North: Both Vul.

	North		
	♠ A 10 9 8 6 2		
	♡ A Q 9 6 5 2		
	◇ —		
	♣ A		

West
♠ K Q J 7 5 4 3
♡ 8 3
◇ 8 7 6 2
♣ —

East
♠ —
♡ —
◇ A Q 10 9 5 3
♣ K Q 10 9 7 6 4

South
♠ —
♡ K J 10 7 4
◇ K J 4
♣ J 8 5 3 2

West	North	East	South
—	1 ♠	2 NT	3 ♡
Pass	6 ♡		

West leads the ◇ 8. Declarer seems to have thirteen tricks on a cross-ruff. Alas, West will ruff the ♣ A, lead a trump and the total will shrink to eleven.

When this hand came up after a goulash—no shuffle and the cards dealt three and four at a time—declarer found a pretty solution. On the ◇ 8 he threw dummy's ♣ A! No return could hurt him.

Now bridge cruising is big business on both sides of the Atlantic and it's growing year by year.

All these events—the Brussels and Monte Carlo money tournaments, Ladbrokes' Individual and Britain's first 'Bridge Congress Afloat'—occurred within weeks of each other. A month or two later, the name of Rothman, the cigarette manufacturers, appeared as sponsors of the European Championships in Ostend.

An astrologer, casting a bridge horoscope for the summer of

1973, would have surely found the planetary signs of commerce very much in the ascendant.

On land and at sea, the sponsors made sure that their promotions were duly publicized. Money speaks in sounds that are loud and clear. Victory points are barely audible and rarely reach the media.

It's true that the World Championships in Bermuda made the front pages—but only because of the sensational accusations of foot-tapping. The scandal was news. The world title wasn't.

No one was accused of cheating later in the year at the European Championships in Brighton, so neither the record entry, nor the victory of the British Ladies over Italy, made much impact. The quality papers mentioned the Championships discreetly. The popular Press ignored the event altogether.

The handful of enthusiasts who subscribed to the daily bulletin from Brighton, edited by Aric Milnes, found in it many fascinating hands.

Take up South's hand, held by Garozzo, in Italy's match against Poland.

Dealer South: Love All

```
                    ♠ 8 6
                    ♡ A 9 8 5
                    ◇ J 10 6
                    ♣ A J 7 3
   ♠ J 9 5 3 2                      ♠ —
   ♡ J 7           ┌─────────┐      ♡ Q 10 6 2
   ◇ 8 7 5         │   N     │      ◇ 9 4 3 2
   ♣ 10 9 8        │ W   E   │      ♣ K Q 6 5 2
                   │   S     │
                   └─────────┘
                    ♠ A K Q 10 7 4
                    ♡ K 4 3
                    ◇ A K Q
                    ♣ 4
```

Someone has overbid, and Benito is in 7 ♠. West leads a club and as dummy goes down, he starts working out how many IMPs he'll lose. Anxiety turns to relief when East shows out on the first rounds of trumps, for against the 5–0 break they won't make 6 ♠ in the other room and the loss will be no more than 100, just three little IMPs.

Alas, it soon becomes apparent that the small slam can be made after all. Garozzo's brow clouds over again as he analyzes the play in 6 ♠.

A club is ruffed at trick two and the ♠ A reveals the cruel trump break. Crossing to the ♡ A, declarer ruffs another club and cashes the ◇ A K Q. West has to follow. Declarer scores his ♡ K and exits with the ♡ 3. Having nothing but trumps left, West has to ruff and lead a trump into the ♠ K Q 10.

Having failed to ruff a club at trick two, Benito went two down, but he needn't have worried. The Poles went three down in 7 NT!

Here's a teaser from Italy's match against Switzerland. How many tricks should South make in 5 ◇ against the best defence? Put down your answer before reading the text below.

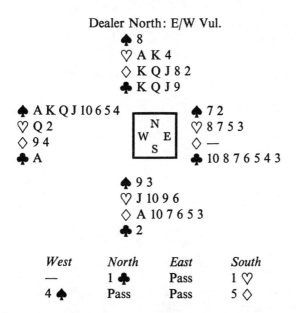

Dealer North: E/W Vul.

```
            ♠ 8
            ♡ A K 4
            ◇ K Q J 8 2
            ♣ K Q J 9
♠ A K Q J 10 6 5 4        ♠ 7 2
♡ Q 2          N           ♡ 8 7 5 3
◇ 9 4       W     E        ◇ —
♣ A            S           ♣ 10 8 7 6 5 4 3
            ♠ 9 3
            ♡ J 10 9 6
            ◇ A 10 7 6 5 3
            ♣ 2
```

West	North	East	South
—	1 ♣	Pass	1 ♡
4 ♠	Pass	Pass	5 ◇

In social bridge, or for that matter, at the club, declarer would surely lose two tricks to the black aces. In an all-star match, West is unlikely to score a trick in spades. Dummy's ♠ 8 should be a winner! And that is what happened.

Pietro Bernasconi, sitting West for Switzerland, led his single-ton ♣ A and realized at once that only a club ruff could beat the contract. But how could he put his partner in? The only hope was to find him with the ♠ 9, so at trick two, Bernasconi underled his five spade honours.

Alas, Italy's Franco had the ♠ 9—and lived happily ever after.

Even at the summit, not every bidding sequence is codified. A refreshing example of the advantages of simplicity over 1 ♣ systems is this hand from Britain's match against Lebanon.

Dealer South: Love All

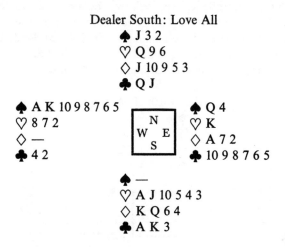

```
                    ♠ J 3 2
                    ♡ Q 9 6
                    ◇ J 10 9 5 3
                    ♣ Q J
  ♠ A K 10 9 8 7 6 5          ♠ Q 4
  ♡ 8 7 2             N        ♡ K
  ◇ —             W     E      ◇ A 7 2
  ♣ 4 2               S        ♣ 10 9 8 7 6 5
                    ♠ —
                    ♡ A J 10 5 4 3
                    ◇ K Q 6 4
                    ♣ A K 3
```

This was the sequence with Britain's Tony Priday, sitting North and Claude Rodrigue, South.

South	West	North	East
2 ♡	4 ♠	5 ♡	5 ♠
6 ♡	6 ♠		

The Lebanese did well to sacrifice, for despite their two aces, the slam in hearts is unbeatable.

In the other room, South opened 1 ♣ and Jeremy Flint, sitting West, called 4 ♠. Having no idea of his partner's distribution, knowing only that he was strong, all North could do was to double.

Jeremy duly wrapped up ten tricks bringing Britain a swing of 13 IMPs.

I sympathize with the reader, who wonders whether experts always execute in practice the plays they know so well in theory. The diagrammed hand, played by Sandelin for Sweden against Iceland, lends itself admirably to a text-book quiz.

Dealer South: Love All

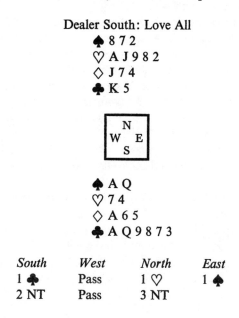

♠ 8 7 2
♡ A J 9 8 2
◇ J 7 4
♣ K 5

N
W E
S

♠ A Q
♡ 7 4
◇ A 6 5
♣ A Q 9 8 7 3

South	West	North	East
1 ♣	Pass	1 ♡	1 ♠
2 NT	Pass	3 NT	

West leads the ♠ 3. How should South play?

ANALYSIS: Declarer needs five club tricks for his contract, which should present no difficulty—if he gives the matter thought.

The 'normal' play is to lead the ♣ 3 up to dummy's ♣ K and . . . . But then nothing matters. Most of the time, all will be well. Occasionally, however, four times in a hundred, declarer will run into the distribution Sandelin found in Brighton.

```
♠ J 5 3              ♠ K 10 9 6 4
♡ K 10 3      N      ♡ Q 6 5
♢ 9 3      W     E    ♢ K Q 10 8 2
♣ J 10 6 4 2    S    ♣ —
```

A sound technician, Sandelin led the ♣ 9 at trick two—and ran it! Next he cashed the ♣ K and coming back with the ♠ A, cleared the clubs.

Two points are worth noting.

It wouldn't have helped West to cover the ♣ 9. And it was safe for Sandelin to use the ♠ A as an entry. If West had a third (or fourth) spade, the suit wasn't dangerous. Alternatively, when he came in, he would have no spade left.

With world champions, Rixi Markus and Fritzi Gordon, back in the team, the British started favourites in the Ladies' Section and won the European in convincing fashion, bringing to an end the four years' reign of the Italians.

The other British pairs were Nicola Gardener and Sandra Landy, Charlie Esterson and Rita Oldroyd. All put up a sterling performance.

Sandra sat South and Nicola North in Britain's match against Austria.

Dealer South: Love All

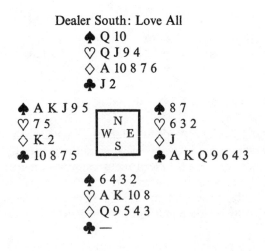

```
                    ♠ Q 10
                    ♡ Q J 9 4
                    ♢ A 10 8 7 6
                    ♣ J 2
♠ A K J 9 5                      ♠ 8 7
♡ 7 5          N           ♡ 6 3 2
♢ K 2       W     E         ♢ J
♣ 10 8 7 5     S            ♣ A K Q 9 6 4 3
                    ♠ 6 4 3 2
                    ♡ A K 10 8
                    ♢ Q 9 5 4 3
                    ♣ —
```

South	*West*	*North*	*East*
1 ◇	1 ♠	Dble	3 ♣
3 ♡	5 ♣	5 ◇	Pass
Pass	Dble		

The bidding is typical of this pair's forceful style.

Though Sandra has only nine high-card points, she may have no way of showing her shapely hand if she doesn't open.

Nicola's double of 1 ♠ is conventional. Known as Sputnik, it guarantees four hearts and at least seven points, but probably more.

Once the heart fit comes to light, Sandra's values shoot up, and though she opened on a sub-minimum, she now has something to spare. Hence the uninhibited bid of 3 ♡.

West cashed the ♠ A K and switched to a club. How should Sandra Landy play the trumps?

Reasoning that West had greater need of the ◇ K than East to justify their respective bids, she led the ◇ Q, catching West's ◇ K and pinning East's ◇ J.

In the other room, they didn't think of 5 ◇.

Britain doesn't win many international events these days, but outside the bridge media, the victory of the Ladies in Brighton passed by almost unnoticed.

In contrast to the lack of publicity for the European Championships was the vibrant coverage in America of the Lancia-sponsored exhibition matches in which Omar Sharif, with the four superstars of the *squadra azzurra*, challenged teams from New York, Los Angeles, Chicago and Miami.

'The Biggest Trophies in History,' cried the headlines. And so they were. Any team that beat Lancia's was to receive five cars worth some 7,000 dollars each. And if, as was only to be expected, Lancia crushed all opponents, those who put up the stiffest resistance would still get five cars. That was a delicate touch.

In the event, the Americans won three of the four matches, losing only in Chicago.

'Omar', quipped Dick Frey, President of the IBPA, 'is Lancia's biggest distributor in the States.'

The most dramatic of the four matches was at Miami where the choice of a single card determined the fate of five Lancias. 'The 35,000 dollar play' was the headline in Ira Corn's syndicated column.

Dealer West: E/W Vul.

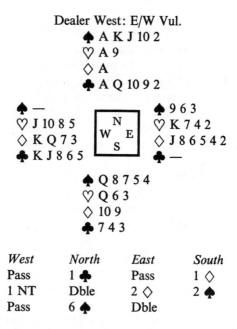

♠ A K J 10 2
♡ A 9
◇ A
♣ A Q 10 9 2

♠ —
♡ J 10 8 5
◇ K Q 7 3
♣ K J 8 6 5

♠ 9 6 3
♡ K 7 4 2
◇ J 8 6 5 4 2
♣ —

♠ Q 8 7 5 4
♡ Q 6 3
◇ 10 9
♣ 7 4 3

West	North	East	South
Pass	1 ♣	Pass	1 ◇
1 NT	Dble	2 ◇	2 ♠
Pass	6 ♠	Dble	

Garozzo's opening 1 ♣ and Sharif's 1 ◇ response were, of course, conventional and so was West's 1 NT, the 'unusual' type, advertising strength in the minors. Benito's values soared at once for now he could expect the club honours to be where he wanted them. Hence the leap to 6 ♠.

Impervious to the lead-directing double, which surely called for a club, West led the ◇ K.

Omar drew trumps, overtaking dummy's ♠ J with his ♠ Q, and successfully negotiated the double finesse in clubs.

Since West, who had passed as dealer, had already shown nine points on a distributional hand, East was pretty well marked with the ♡ K. Omar Sharif laid down the ♡ A and continued with the ♡ 9. Without a care in the world, or so it seemed, John Mohan, sitting East, followed smoothly with the ♡ 4.

Omar paused in his tracks.

Did that young Californian really have the ♡ K? Could he be so nonchalant, so brazen?

Omar Sharif decided that Mohan looked altogether too innocent and that his only chance was to drop a doubleton ♡ K. So he played low, lost the trick to West's ♡ 10—and five Lancias with it. The slam was no longer makeable and the hand decided the match.

Big bridge sponsors, in addition to those mentioned already, include Philip Morris, the tobacco giants, Cutty Sark Whisky and hotel chains in several countries.

In terms of value for money, Bols, the Dutch gin and liqueur manufacturers, brought off a coup with their Bridge Tips Competition launched through the *Bulletin* of the International Bridge Press Association. Eight champions of world renown were invited to give the average player a word of advice, outlining a favourite stratagem, stressing this or that point in technique, with a diagram to illustrate it.

The tips were excellent copy for bridge journalists, nearly all of whom take the *Bulletin*. What could be more convenient than to be offered a ready-made article with a big name to back it? Every Bols tip was reproduced in bridge columns throughout the world and everyone was happy—the readers, who were presented with interesting hands; the journalists, who were spared a lot of work; and Bols, who received a lot of publicity.

This was the entry from Giorgio Belladonna, whose theme was —the ace of trumps. Not only is it worth a certain trick, but played at the *right time* it can be worth two or three tricks, as here:

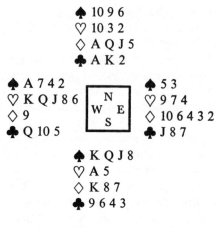

CONTRACT 4 ♠ : LEAD ♡ K

South takes the trick and leads trumps. If West wins the first or second time, the contract is unbeatable. Declarer throws a club on the third heart, and claims the rest.

If, however, West holds up his ♠ A twice, the contract is un-makeable. Should South lead a third trump, West will win and force declarer in hearts, gaining trump control. If South doesn't lead another trump, West will live to ruff a diamond.

The play which appeals especially to the Brazilian star, Gabriel Chagas, is the intra-finesse. It is in two stages—a finesse against one honour, then a second finesse against another, opposite, scooping the first one, as here:

Dealer East: E/W Vul.

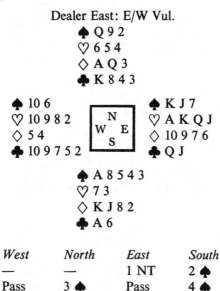

♠ Q 9 2
♡ 6 5 4
◇ A Q 3
♣ K 8 4 3

♠ 10 6   ♠ K J 7
♡ 10 9 8 2   ♡ A K Q J
◇ 5 4   ◇ 10 9 7 6
♣ 10 9 7 5 2   ♣ Q J

♠ A 8 5 4 3
♡ 7 3
◇ K J 8 2
♣ A 6

West	North	East	South
—	—	1 NT	2 ♠
Pass	3 ♠	Pass	4 ♠

West leads the ♡ 10. South expects East to have the ♠ K, so after ruffing the third round of hearts, he embarks on an intra-finesse.

He leads the ♠ 4, inserting dummy's ♠ 9 and losing to East's ♠ J. Winning the club return, he cashes his second top club and ruffs a third club to get a picture of the distribution. When East shows out, he decides to play him for three trumps and West for a doubleton. So he crosses to the ◇ A and plays his ♠ Q, finessing against East's ♠ K and smothering West's ♠ 10.

A panel of experts adjudged Terence Reese to be the winner of the competition and of the first prize of 1,000 dollars. Reese's tip was: 'Study the early discards and consider—from what holding would defender most readily have made those discards?'

He gave this example:

Dealer South: Love All

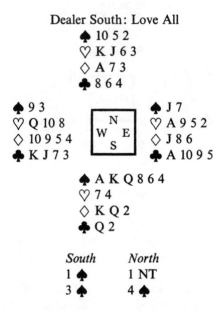

```
                    ♠ 10 5 2
                    ♡ K J 6 3
                    ◇ A 7 3
                    ♣ 8 6 4
  ♠ 9 3                              ♠ J 7
  ♡ Q 10 8           N              ♡ A 9 5 2
  ◇ 10 9 5 4      W     E           ◇ J 8 6
  ♣ K J 7 3          S              ♣ A 10 9 5
                    ♠ A K Q 8 6 4
                    ♡ 7 4
                    ◇ K Q 2
                    ♣ Q 2
```

South	*North*
1 ♠	1 NT
3 ♠	4 ♠

West leads the ♣ 3. Ruffing the third round of clubs, declarer plays four rounds of trumps, keeping dummy's hearts intact. West throws a club and a diamond, East a club and a heart.

After cashing the diamonds, declarer leads a heart, and West follows with the ♡ 8. Which heart should South play from dummy?

The ♡ J, says Reese.

Why? Because of East's heart discard. With four hearts to the ace, expecting the contract to depend on the heart guess, he could afford to discard one. Not so with four hearts to the queen, for if declarer had the ♡ A he could set up a heart by ruffing.

When East discards, the ◇ A is still in dummy, of course, as an entry.

I estimate the cost to Bols of the entire competition, including all the prizes and administrative expenses in 1974–5, at not more than 7,000 dollars. A bargain. Not surprisingly, Bols came back for more, offering bigger prizes, the next season.

The infusion of so much money into bridge and the attendant publicity cannot fail to stimulate interest. But is it an unmixed blessing?

A survey carried out among members of the International Bridge Press Association showed a general expectation that money tournaments would soon dominate the scene in America, as in Europe. Nearly 70 per cent welcomed the prospect. Only 25 per cent were against it, the rest expressing no opinion.

I confess that I voted with the minority. The lure of money will, I fear, turn many amateurs into professionals, which will be bad for bridge and worse still for the erstwhile amateurs.

What is a professional?

In Europe the term usually describes a good player who earns his livelihood by winning money from bad ones. The occupation is neither widespread nor lucrative.

It's very different in America. There, money bridge isn't as popular as it is in Europe, but many third-rate performers in the States are imbued with an urge to prove—to themselves if to no one else—that they are really second-rate. And what proof could be more compelling than the accumulation of master points? Success is certain. All it needs is the time to play and the money to hire good partners.

This may be ridiculous, but it's relatively harmless. The evil comes about when a rich sponsor buys up a whole team so as to play in it himself. This is coming in for increasing criticism in America.

The objection is not to the practice itself, but to the consequences it may have in international events.

The team with the best record in the Spingold and the Vanderbilt, the two main tournaments, usually represents America in the World Championship. Can it afford to carry a member who is playing out of his class?

An article under the Goren byline in *Sports Illustrated*, arguing that it can't, gives this example from the finals of the Spingold in 1973.

Dealer South: N/S Vul.

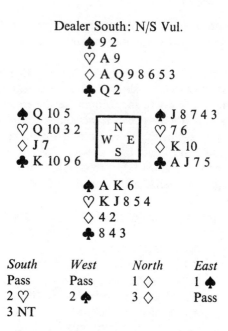

```
                    ♠ 9 2
                    ♡ A 9
                    ◇ A Q 9 8 6 5 3
                    ♣ Q 2
  ♠ Q 10 5                         ♠ J 8 7 4 3
  ♡ Q 10 3 2          N            ♡ 7 6
  ◇ J 7            W     E         ◇ K 10
  ♣ K 10 9 6          S            ♣ A J 7 5
                    ♠ A K 6
                    ♡ K J 8 5 4
                    ◇ 4 2
                    ♣ 8 4 3
```

South	West	North	East
Pass	Pass	1 ◇	1 ♠
2 ♡	2 ♠	3 ◇	Pass
3 NT			

West led the ♠ 5. Declarer won with the ♠ A and led the ◇ 2, inserting dummy's ◇ 9. East won. What should he have played? The expert has no problem.

Clearly South has the ♠ K and will reel off nine tricks as soon as he gains the lead, unless defenders can seize four more tricks quickly. Clubs offer the only chance.

Alas, East was the rich sponsor and returned unthinkingly another spade. Declarer claimed later that he took the deep finesse in diamonds, to cater for a bare ◇ K, because he felt sure that East wouldn't find the right defence.

Charles and Katherine Wei deserve a mention in this connection. 'C.C.', as he is often called, could buy his way into half a dozen top teams without mortgaging a single tanker. The thought has never crossed his mind.

Katherine doesn't have to use her cheque-book to play with experts for she is one in her own right. For all that, though she has captained the Blue Team more than once—always successfully —she doesn't supplement IMPs with dollars to play out of her class.

As a player, she has many achievements to her credit, but none so striking as her performance in 1973 when she drove relentlessly through America's top-seeded teams to reach the finals of the Vanderbilt Cup.

She is South here:

Dealer South: Both Vul.

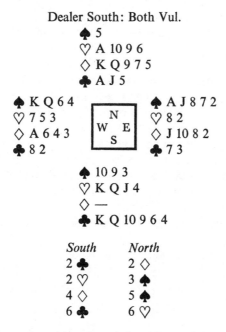

```
                  ♠ 5
                  ♡ A 10 9 6
                  ◇ K Q 9 7 5
                  ♣ A J 5
  ♠ K Q 6 4                    ♠ A J 8 7 2
  ♡ 7 5 3          N           ♡ 8 2
  ◇ A 6 4 3    W     E         ◇ J 10 8 2
  ♣ 8 2            S           ♣ 7 3
                  ♠ 10 9 3
                  ♡ K Q J 4
                  ◇ —
                  ♣ K Q 10 9 6 4
```

South	North
2 ♣	2 ◇
2 ♡	3 ♠
4 ◇	5 ♠
6 ♣	6 ♡

The 2 ♣ opening shows length in clubs and less than sixteen points, the minimum for the Precision 1 ♣. In response to North's 2 ◇, asking about distribution, Katherine shows her hearts, her second suit. Thereafter, an exchange of cue-bids establishes the first- and second-round controls in diamonds and in spades, allowing an unbeatable slam to be reached on a mere twenty-five count. Not a single point in either hand is wasted. All 'work'.

The unhappy corollary of the surge forward of the money interest is the fading out of events with a social background, in which money plays no part. A sad example is the demise of the Devonshire Club's Rubber Bridge Tournament, one of the most enjoyable competitions in the bridge calendar.

The origin of this event goes back to the pre-war days of gracious living when the Portland Club inaugurated a tournament that was in many ways unique.

Marrying rubber bridge to duplicate, the hands were pre-dealt, duplicated and played simultaneously in both rooms. When the rubber was over in one room, play stopped in both and the scores were added up, the losers taking 300 for game.

A feature of the competition, strictly confined to London's famous social clubs, was the dinner at half-time. Good food, good wine and witty toasts induced a mellow, convivial atmosphere rarely found in other bridge events.

During the war, the Portland discontinued the competition and in 1946 the Devonshire Club took up the torch to carry on the happy tradition.

There was gaiety and panache about the game, especially after the post-prandial toasts, but also plenty of good carefree bridge.

Several teams had internationals, but all included ordinary players without a master point to their names.

Card clubs, like Crockfords, were not eligible.

My own club, the Royal Automobile, won the tournament eleven times.

This was a hand in one of our matches against Hurlingham:

Dealer West: N/S Game

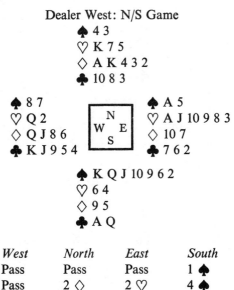

♠ 4 3
♡ K 7 5
◇ A K 4 3 2
♣ 10 8 3

♠ 8 7
♡ Q 2
◇ Q J 8 6
♣ K J 9 5 4

♠ A 5
♡ A J 10 9 8 3
◇ 10 7
♣ 7 6 2

♠ K Q J 10 9 6 2
♡ 6 4
◇ 9 5
♣ A Q

West	North	East	South
Pass	Pass	Pass	1 ♠
Pass	2 ◇	2 ♡	4 ♠

The bidding and the defence were the same in both rooms. The ♡ Q was led. East forced declarer with a third heart and again, when he came in with the ♠ A, hoping to promote a trump for West. South could afford to ruff high and it looked as if all would hinge on the club finesse. One South tried it and went down. The other reasoned that with the ♣ K, as well as six good hearts and the ♠ A, East wouldn't have passed originally. So he laid down the ♣ A and reeled off his trumps. On the last one West had to unguard the diamonds or throw the ♣ K.

Like so many good things, club life has been on the decline for many years. The murky waters of progress, lapping around the old world, haven't spared the Devonshire and 1974 saw the last of the tournaments for their Cup.

An instructive hand came up in the final in which the Law Society defeated the Constitutional Club. Louis Tarlo for the winners and Alfred Cohen for the losers played the same way.

Dealer South: N/S Vul.

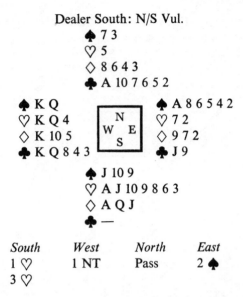

```
                    ♠ 7 3
                    ♡ 5
                    ◇ 8 6 4 3
                    ♣ A 10 7 6 5 2
♠ K Q                   ┌─────┐              ♠ A 8 6 5 4 2
♡ K Q 4                 │  N  │              ♡ 7 2
◇ K 10 5              W │     │ E            ◇ 9 7 2
♣ K Q 8 4 3             │  S  │              ♣ J 9
                        └─────┘
                    ♠ J 10 9
                    ♡ A J 10 9 8 6 3
                    ◇ A Q J
                    ♣ —
```

South	West	North	East
1 ♡	1 NT	Pass	2 ♠
3 ♡			

West begins with the ♠ K Q and switches to the ♣ K. Declarer goes up with dummy's ♣ A, discarding a diamond, ruffs a club and leads the ♠ J.

West is helpless. If he discards a club or diamond, South ruffs, trumps a club in his hand and exits with the ♡ J.

Coming in with one of his honours, West can struggle on for one more trick by leading the ♣ Q. South ruffs, and now the ♡ A, followed by another trump, forces West to lead a diamond into South's ◇ A Q or a club to dummy's ♣ 10.

West does no better by ruffing the ♠ J.

Just as there seems to be no place in the modern world for the pleasant *insouciance* of the Devonshire Cup, so a cold wind has set in for the annual Oxford and Cambridge match. This, too, goes back many years and has a social background.

The match, always played in London, was followed by a gala dinner, with black ties *de rigueur*, at a West End hotel. More recently it was a West End club, then a club in Hampstead.

In 1975 the card manufacturing company which had sponsored the event, withdrew its support, and the tournament, traditionally held in April, had to be postponed.

Sensation rather than science characterized the 1974 match. There were never more than 20 IMPs between the two sides and the result, a close win for Oxford, was in doubt until the end.

On one dramatic set of boards, Oxford brought home a vulnerable grand slam, missing two aces—and Cambridge gained 16 IMPs!

Dealer South: Both Vul.

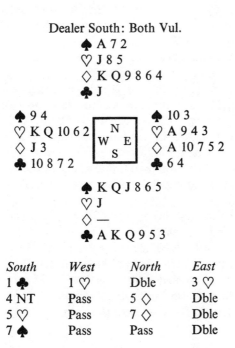

♠ A 7 2
♡ J 8 5
◇ K Q 9 8 6 4
♣ J

♠ 9 4
♡ K Q 10 6 2
◇ J 3
♣ 10 8 7 2

♠ 10 3
♡ A 9 4 3
◇ A 10 7 5 2
♣ 6 4

♠ K Q J 8 6 5
♡ J
◇ —
♣ A K Q 9 5 3

South	West	North	East
1 ♣	1 ♡	Dble	3 ♡
4 NT	Pass	5 ◇	Dble
5 ♡	Pass	7 ◇	Dble
7 ♠	Pass	Pass	Dble

North's double of 1 ♡ was Sputnik, though hardly in the classical tradition. East's raise to 3 ♡ came nearest to a normal bid in an Alice in Wonderland sequence. Few hands with a void qualify for Blackwood and South's surely isn't one of them. Neither is it clear what he meant by 5 ♡. Was it intended to inhibit a heart lead? It certainly had that effect for West led the ◇ J, setting up a diamond trick to take care of South's heart loser.

Though the bidding may have been erratic, the spirit in which the match was played was, as always, wholly admirable.

Alas, there was no money in it.

But there was money galore in whisky, and the Maginot Line against commercialism was well and truly turned the following year when one of the English Bridge Union's main events, the autumn congress at Eastbourne, shed its white virginal robes to emerge brazenly in scarlet as the Cutty Sark Festival of Bridge.

Launched nearly thirty years earlier, the prizes had always been nominal. Now, an impressive list included objects of value and two expensive cruises.

How long would it be, asked the cynics, before money replaced master-points as the main attraction?

Every story should have a happy ending and this is no exception. The Curzon House Group, which controls some of London's best-known casinos, came to the rescue of Oxford and Cambridge, and the annual match was held in the luxurious surroundings of Curzon House. And the following year saw a revival of the Devonshire Cup with the Oxford and Cambridge Club acting as hosts.

My last hand will highlight an old theme in a new setting. The year is 1975.

To the ancient cry 'Peers versus People', the two Houses of Parliament send their champions to the Chelsea Hotel in Knightsbridge to do battle on a field of green baize. No coronets, no mace, no despatch box. Aces and kings are the chosen weapons and the rules of combat follow the pattern of the Devonshire Cup, combining rubber bridge and duplicate.

Declarer here is Sir Harwood Harrison.

Dealer South: N/S Vul.

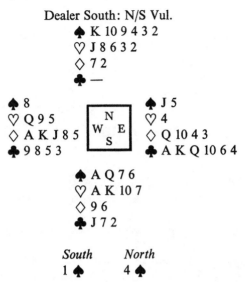

♠ K 10 9 4 3 2
♡ J 8 6 3 2
♢ 7 2
♣ —

♠ 8   ♠ J 5
♡ Q 9 5   ♡ 4
♢ A K J 8 5   ♢ Q 10 4 3
♣ 9 8 5 3   ♣ A K Q 10 6 4

♠ A Q 7 6
♡ A K 10 7
♢ 9 6
♣ J 7 2

South	*North*
1 ♠	4 ♠

Sir Harwood had no trouble, of course, in wrapping up ten tricks. And yet, the hand belonged to the Lords, who could have made 5 ♣ or 5 ♢.

East had almost the ideal hand to come in with 4 NT, calling on partner to show his longer minor. Little risk was involved, especially at favourable vulnerability. After North's jump to 4 ♠ it was clear that West could have at most two spades and therefore at least eleven non-spades. So he was likely to have a four- or five-card minor. Even if he had three cards in both, no disaster could occur.

The Lords, trailing at half-time, won a closely fought match. The following year the Commons had their revenge. And as both Houses sharpened their weapons for the next encounter, a new tradition was born.

Finale

Five fateful years drew rapidly to a close.

The world over, old values collapsed and ancient institutions crumbled.

Abroad, Cuban conquistadors in Russian armour were on the rampage in Africa.

At home, proclaiming sex equality, Parliament enacted that though men might not be women, women were, to all intents and purposes, men. Proud sterling plummeted and terrorist bombs, and warnings of more bombs, became a feature of life in London.

The impossible was happening every day.

When beggars die there are no comets seen. In 1976 all the signs and portents heralded the dawn of a new age, and on a sunny May day in Monte Carlo, it happened.

The Italian phoenix bowed to the American eagles and after twenty glorious years the reign of the Blue Team ended. The invincibles had been vanquished in the world championship and the Bermuda Bowl, symbol of bridge supremacy, went back once more across the Atlantic.

An era had come to an end.